791·43

D1792681

The American Film Institute Monograph Series

Ann Martin
Supervising Editor

CINEMA HISTORIES
CINEMA PRACTICES

Edited by

Patricia Mellencamp
and
Philip Rosen

University Publications of America, Inc.

Copyright © The American Film Institute 1984

LCCN 83-22457
ISBN 0-89093-571-1 (pbk.)

The American Film Institute *Monograph* Series is published by University Publications of America, Inc., Frederick, MD, in association with The American Film Institute.

The American Film Institute
2021 North Western Avenue
P.O. Box 27999
Los Angeles, California 90027

Library of Congress Cataloging in Publication Data

Cinema histories, cinema practices.

(The American Film Institute monograph series ; v. 4)
Includes bibliographical references.
1. Moving-picture plays—History and criticism—
Addresses, essays, lectures. I. Mellencamp, Patricia.
II. Rosen, Philip. III. Series.
PN1995.C497   1984   791.43   83-22457
ISBN 0-89093-571-1 (pbk.)

Table of Contents

Contributors

EDWARD BRANIGAN, an attorney in Los Angeles, has taught film at the University of California at Los Angeles and is currently Visiting Assistant Professor at the University of Iowa. He is the author of *Point of View in the Cinema* as well as articles in *Screen, Film Reader, Wide Angle, Wisconsin Law Review* and *Comm/ent*.

EDWARD BUSCOMBE is General Editor in the Publishing Department of the British Film Institute. He has been on the editorial boards of both *Screen* and *Screen Education*. He is currently working on a study of the Western.

MANUEL DE LANDA moved to New York City in 1975 after studying design in Mexico City. He works in the special effects department of a film production company, and is well-known as an independent avant-garde filmmaker. His research extends to the philosophy of language and linguistics.

THOMAS ELSAESSER teaches English and film at the University of East Anglia. Former Editor of *Monogram*, he has contributed to *Screen, Positif, Ciné-Tracts, New German Critique, Wide Angle, October* and other journals. In the United States he has taught at the University of Iowa, and the University of California at Los Angeles and at Santa Barbara.

PETER LEHMAN is Associate Professor of Film in the Department of Drama at the University of Arizona, and co-author, with William Luhr, of *Blake Edwards* and *Authorship and Narrative in the Cinema*.

PATRICIA MELLENCAMP teaches film history and theory in the Art History Department of the University of Wisconsin-Milwaukee. She has written articles on the musical and avant-garde film for *Ciné-Tracts*, and is the co-editor, with Stephen Heath, of *Cinema and Language*, and, with Mary Ann Doane and Linda Williams, of *Re-vision: Essays in Feminist Film Criticism*.

PHILIP ROSEN is Director of the Screen Studies Program at Clark University. He has written articles on film theory which have appeared in a number of journals including *October*, *Quarterly Review of Film Studies*, *Screen* and *Yale French Studies*.

MICHAEL SILVERMAN teaches in the Semiotics Program at Brown University. He is co-author, with Carl Klaus and Robert Scholes, of *Elements of Literature and Film*, and has published film theory and criticism in such journals as *American Film*, *Ciné-Tracts*, *Film Quarterly* and *Yale French Studies*.

MAUREEN TURIM teaches in the Cinema Department at SUNY-Binghamton. She has published articles in *Wide Angle*, *Enclitic* and *Semiotica*, and is currently working on her book entitled *Flashbacks in Films: Memory Processes and the Subjectivity of History*.

ANDREW TYNDALL is a British filmmaker based in New York City. His work includes *Argument* (made with Anthony McCall), and he was a member of the collective which made *Sigmund Freud's Dora*.

Introduction

Patricia Mellencamp
and
Philip Rosen

Part I of this volume, 'Cinema Histories,' includes essays which focus on questions associated with film history: problems of temporal change and stasis in film styles, forms and subject matter; problems of economic and social determinations which shaped film practices during specific historical periods, etc. Part II, 'Cinema Practices,' presents diverse papers which focus on questions associated with the theoretical or practical axis of mainstream/ classical versus alternative/avant-garde cinemas. The two sections are only separated for convenience, for it will be clear that beyond the explicit questions posed in individual papers, their concerns intersect across the division between histories and practices. It is obvious that the 'mainstream-alternative' opposition is critical to any conception of film history; equally, a historical position seems implicit in any notion of classical or avant-garde practices.

In addition, a more fundamental intersection is operative. All the writers share an awareness and knowledge of (if not necessarily a complete allegiance to) a conceptual framework which has influenced Anglo-American film studies since the early 1970s. This theoretical frame (sometimes loosely labeled 'structuralist' or 'post-structuralist') conceives of the textual operations of films in terms derived in large part from the writings of Saussure, Peirce, Freud, Lévi-Strauss, Lacan, Althusser, Derrida, Barthes and/or Foucault. While this theoretical impulse is not unique to film studies, there has been an especially strong tendency in this discipline to deflect it in a particular direction: towards the project of comprehending cinema as an *institution* or a multiplicity of institutional practices.

Such an investigation has broad ramifications. Because the central question is exactly what is being *instituted* over a wide terrain of, for example, filmic textuality, specific instances will be invoked as examples of more general practices. More specifically, the definitions of general practices have entailed claims about social organization. Indeed, it is tautological to say that an institution is a *social* entity. In analyzing institutions, one is examining organizational structures and practices which encompass individual agents (or texts) and which in part bind individuals together in a social cohesion. Thus it is not surprising that this approach ultimately has important political implications. Because many scholars originally attracted to structuralist and post-structuralist analyses of film were seeking fresh models of culture compatible with leftist perspectives, it is also not surprising that several of the essays in this collection discuss cinema and history in relation to recent Marxist theoretical developments.

One central example of the achievements and generalizing influence of this current of structuralist and post-structuralist analysis of cinema is what has been called a 'theory of the subject' in relation to specifically filmic textual processes. This construct has founded a sophisticated, psychoanalytically-based theory and criticism in which 'film is not a static and isolated object but a series of relations with the spectator it imagines, plays, and sets as subject in its movement.'[1] This conception could be developed in a number of ways pertaining to a social and/or political view of culture in general and cinema in particular. For example, it has been productive (and has also resulted in complex controversies) to examine classical cinema for the 'visual pleasure' its textual mechanisms produce. It has been forcibly argued that a classical paradigm of textual strategies can be read as engaging (and hence positing) a male spectating subject who derives satisfaction from configurations of voyeurism and fetishism.[2] Indeed, the argument that cinema is an institution which posits a unified spectating subject in need of constant psychic reassurance and ceaseless reconfirmation of identity has been one of the most fruitful hypotheses in the history of thinking about cinema.

Nevertheless, no such general conceptual framework can or should go unopposed. Critiques of widely varying seriousness and importance, deriving from differing perspectives, have been advanced. In addition, important critiques, revisions and modifications have been staged *within* this theoretical problematic. Of particular relevance here are positions challenging the very power, the totalizing generality, of certain of the most influential formulations. Sometimes the cinematic apparatus, or narrative, is described in such all-encompassing terms that it becomes difficult to make distinctions among different kinds of films. Thus arise the crucial issues of specific forms of significations, of diversified types of cinematic institutions and modes of spectatorship.

The contributions to this volume define and engage areas of inquiry in which such specificity could be sought. Several zones of contention are suggested by the various essays. First, given the framework sketched above, is it possible to conceptualize historical specificity? If so, rather than studying *the* cinematic institution, research would scrutinize filmic institution*s* within the multiple institutions (e.g., of visual pleasure) of different societies, with sensitivity to the possibility of historical shifts in institutions. Hence, to seek historical specificities of the cinematic institution is to sublate the concept of cinematic specificity according to the relations cinema holds with non-cinematic institutions and practices.

A second area of concern is whether it is possible to investigate mainstream cinema and alternative cinema in ways that explain their implications in specific situations—e.g., the practical, political and textual work of distribution/exhibition-reception/use. In the end, this question is fundamentally inseparable from the first question of historical specificity.

It is significant and not coincidental that in this volume these issues are addressed by historians, theorists and filmmakers—three categories of activity so often separated by the academic division of labor. No matter what one's theoretical, aesthetic and/or ideological proclivity, the general questions addressed in this volume will not vanish. This is true not only for the study of cinema but for all institutional practices—including art, media, communications and culture.

Finally, it may be useful to conclude with a beginning, a brief 'history' of this collection of essays—one document, one written and selective trace of a collective event. Original versions of the contributions to this anthology were presented at 'Cinema Histories, Cinema Practices I,' a conference sponsored by the Center for the Humanities at the University of Southern California, and held in May, 1981, in California. (In many ways, the event was an accumulation of effects of six previous film theory events held since 1976 at the Center for Twentieth Century Studies, University of Wisconsin-Milwaukee.) The project's initial document was the following conference announcement, predicated in large part on the writings of Michel Foucault, a delimitation not singularly or simply adhered to by the participants. The approach does, however, foreshadow the overtone of certain essays.

*   *   *

The 'Hollywood System' of film production, distribution and exhibition, a profit-maximizing machine, was perfected, it is argued by some film historians, by Adolph Zukor at Paramount, copied by the other major studios, and exported intact to every non-socialist country in the world from the 1920s on. Its assumptions and film texts are embedded in most current theoretical writings, e.g., Christian Metz and Jean-Louis Baudry. The pleasurable exchange of this modeled narrative and its figurations is profitable, sometimes, for industry executives as well as film theorists. These narratives have overwhelmed film history as well, resulting characteristically in a pastiche of further fictions. Distribution, exhibition/reception (from sleazy storefronts to picture palaces to shopping centers serving six to sixteen simultaneous narratives with ever-growing buckets of popcorn) are historically critical and variable elements of cinema's air-conditioned, anonymously dark pleasure package; but the facts—and their consequences—of the circulation of films within or between cultures are poorly understood.

Emergences of 'national cinemas' (a loose, easy, and inaccurate label)—e.g., Soviet, 1930; Italian, 1940; French, 1950; Polish, 1960; German, 1920 and 1970—usually through state-supported national film schools or studios, are hailed and consumed by critics, historians and audiences, conscribed within a brief social aberration (such as the Russian Revolution) by other scholars, then dismissed. Hollywood either imports its competitors or floods other nations' screens with the U.S. narrative model. Academics also erase other practices by conscription. The economic-political-social histories of these interventions, their alternative and historically specific forms of production and circulation, are largely unwritten, haphazardly covered-up by the romantic assumptions of the term 'art'—a series of stylistic movements led by embattled geniuses. Too often, the assignment of authorship and chronology conceals the lack of, or need for, histories which might offer more sophisticated explanations of the socioeconomic and symbolic nature of this pervasive cultural form.

Against, or because of, narrative cinemas and their institutions (importantly including the conception of a universal, timeless, classless audience) is waged the economic struggle of avant-garde cinemas—variously labeled 'visionary,' 'independent,' 'personal,' or 'experimental.' In the beginning . . . coexistent with narrative in the films of the Lumière Brothers; made spectacular and shocking by the French avant-gardes of the 20s; aligning itself with non-literary artistic traditions in the 60s and 70s, avant-garde cinemas posed alternative 'ways of seeing,' often breaking both the marriage of sound and image as well as the heterosexual couple, cinema's narrative/ marital contract with audiences. Inevitably, art history repeats itself. The history of these interventions assigns authorship (genius usually) or ranks the films as high or higher 'art.' Consideration of the variant terms of production and alternative patterns of use and circulation among specified audiences is rare in historical or theoretical accounts of avant-garde cinema. Rather, the film/maker is fetish-ized, patron-ized by governments, universities, foundations and critics, rarely polemicized or analyzed.

With few exceptions, the political and economic 'unseen' (because off-screen) remains unwritten.

*Refer discourse not to the
thought, to the mind, or to the
object which might have given
rise to it, but to the practical field
in which it is deployed.*
—Michel Foucault

History, like power, looks for ever more perfect 'truths.' Whether discovered on stone tablets, in the brains of 'geniuses,' or as technological 'firsts,' this ontological impulse belongs to the historian as well as to the priest. This version of historical writing, coupled with 'the dominance of the visible' in Western representations, has funneled cinema's history into a narrow corner, with newly published voices repetitiously intoning fabled anecdotes, resuscitating the same facts and films which, in these stories, slip without intercession or variation onto theater screens. This history is as magical as Méliès.

Against this alchemical wizardry, cinema's history can be examined as a competition/collaboration of discrete discourses, operating at specific historical moments within political and social contexts. Discourses of law, business, publicity and technology, spiced by gossip and personal remembrances, weave complex webs around films, yet have been collated as a singular entity, whose only discourse is contained in the film text. The extra-textual conditions of production, distribution and exhibition/reception have largely been relegated to either a footnote or an afterthought. *The initial step of this project is to reexamine the premises of cinema histories*, the history *of* cinema, history *in* cinema and cinema *as* history. This will involve an interchange between scholars and practitioners in order productively to open this terrain, hampered by the inaccessibility or decomposition of primary documents and layered with a fifty-year accumulation of mythology as 'fact.'

In a parallel course, alternative practices, whether labeled 'independent,' 'experimental,' or 'national,' have been analyzed by a constant superimposition of a dominant, fictive model over films in a point/counterpoint composition. Lost in this reductive process have been the variant economic, cultural and artistic terms of production and circulation. *The second goal of this project involves analyses of specific film practices*, including, for example, definitions of the concepts 'independent' and 'avant-garde,' reconstructions of film movements (not merely citations of stylistic idiosyncrasies), histories of surrounding technologies and their incorporation into cinema, e.g., optical printers and video.

Inextricable from the two previous objectives is the scrutiny of the conjunctures between theory, politics and film practices (e.g., Paris, 1968; writings of Metz through Freud/Lacan; and Hollywood films). These intersections are often not chronological or 'national,' resulting in notions of transcultural juxtapositions and alternative readings. These histories should be contextualized by other approaches and findings, for example, anthropological, sociological, and economic.

The final, cumulative move in this gameplay will be the creation of theoretical constructs which can begin to encompass this historical complex of stories, flickering grains/colors/sound/lights, human bodies, law suits, agents/producers/directors/studios/conglomerates, and popcorn, labeled 'going to the movies.'

Critical to all the topic areas is the impetus toward reexamination and the positing of new theoretical models provided by feminist critiques of cinema's institutions and written and filmed texts. This project will analyze women's essentially erased 'places' in the industries—whether that place be a home in Colorado or the Freed Unit at MGM. These stories are rarely told, barely remembered. It is becoming glaringly apparent that historians must engage the problems of sexual difference as well as theoreticians; this is an essential task.

Patricia Mellencamp
April, 1980

＊　　＊　　＊

Questions of feminism did intersect the entire topic. However, the papers which explicitly centered on feminist issues were contextualized by additional essays and printed in a separate AFI Monograph, *Re-vision: Essays in Feminist Film Criticism*, this book's companion volume. This division for publication purposes is not a replication of the conference structure or debates, where a strong feminist component was evident in discussions of historiography and avant-garde practices. Indeed, those papers had an impact on many of the final versions of the essays included here, all initially presented during the conference.

We hope that some degree of the energy of the debates of four intensive days in Monterey slips through in this selection—only one record of many critical positions. So that their participation does not disappear without at least a brief trace, we gratefully acknowledge the presentations and interventions of Robert C. Allen, Nick Browne, Steve Fagin, Raymond Fielding, Lucy Fischer, Sylvia Harvey, Brian Henderson, Jim Hoberman, Beverle Houston, E. Ann Kaplan, Marsha Kinder, Ron Levaco, Colin McArthur, Anthony McCall, Dana Polan, Paul Sharits and others we might have overlooked. The active interventions of film historians Garth Jowett and Gerald Mast, who did not share many of the assumptions outlined in this introduction, were significant elements of the discussions and controversies.

We have been fortunate to have the collaboration of the very talented Ann Martin, our extraordinary editor at The American Film Institute. We are indebted for typing assistance from the Clark University Word Processing Center and the Department of Art History at the University of Wisconsin-Milwaukee.

Finally and most importantly, we acknowledge the constant tactical, creative efforts of Ron Gottesman, Director of the Center for the Humanities at the University of Southern California. He put all the pieces together, including the funding, partially provided by the National Endowment for the Arts. As the engaging, witty Master of Debated Ceremonies, he generously supplied both the intellectual and physical facilities for the gathering. This indefatigable organizer, scholar and veteran campaigner for the serious study of cinema once again deserves great credit and our grateful thanks.

NOTES

1. Stephen Heath, 'Narrative Space,' in *Questions of Cinema* (London: Macmillan & Co., 1981), p. 52.

2. The most concise—and already classic—statement of this view is by Laura Mulvey in her influential essay 'Visual Pleasure and Narrative Cinema' (*Screen*, vol. 16, no. 3 [1975], pp. 6-18). Discussion, debate and developments stemming from this article constitute a good-sized bibliography. For some of the implications, see the third AFI Monograph, *Re-vision: Essays in Feminist Film Criticism* (Los Angeles, CA: The American Film Institute, 1983).

I

CINEMA HISTORIES

Bread and Circuses:
Economics and the Cinema

Edward Buscombe

The nature of our intelligence is such that it is stimulated far less by the will to know than by the will to understand, and, from this, it results that the only sciences which it admits to be authentic are those which succeed in establishing explanatory relationships between phenomena. The rest is, as Malebranche put it, mere 'polymathy.' Now, polymathy can well assume the form either of recreation or of mania, but it cannot today, any more than in the time of Malebranche, pass for one of the proper tasks of the intellect. Even apart from any application of conduct, history will rightfully claim its place among those sciences truly worthy of endeavor only in proportion as it promises us, not simply a disjointed and, you might say, a nearly infinite enumeration, but a rational classification and progressive intelligibility.[1]

These words of Marc Bloch, one of the founders of the *Annales* school of history, retain a pertinence for film history, where the making of lists, of films made, films seen, films 'discovered,' continues to exert a peculiar fascination. Yet it would be untrue to assert that we have no explanatory models. One in particular remains influential, that which offers an account of a determining relationship between economic forces and cultural products. For while there are now signs of a reaction against the domination which Marxist theory has seemed to exercise over film studies (I say 'seemed' because that domination has been wielded with security only in a few isolated citadels, managing merely the occasional foraging raid into the rich flatlands of established academic practice, while in the wastelands inhabited by newspaper film reviewers its decrees were reduced to the sound of distant warcries; and because, to switch metaphors, while Marxism may have set the pace, some who were up with the pacemakers were perhaps only slipstreaming), the question of economic determinacy is still obstinately there on the agenda. Nor is it easy to see how it could be otherwise where the cinema is concerned. In a medium where money is so palpably present at every point in the chain of production and circulation, the effect of the economic ought surely to be demonstrable: for if not in cinema then where?

It hardly needs saying that the complexities of the relationship between the economic and the production of symbolic structures or, more generally, ideology, cannot be encompassed in a short paper. Colin MacCabe has said that 'The main problem facing anyone wishing to articulate a theory of film within a Marxist theory of ideology is that by and large no such Marxist theory exists.'[2] It would be more strictly accurate, perhaps, to say that Marx himself did not produce such a theory. His own pronouncements on this question were suggestive, but a long way short of exhaustive. For while he certainly believed that economics determined ideology, the precise details of that relationship were never filled out with the massive, concrete documentation he supplied for his description of the forces and relations of production within the economy itself. As a result, Marxists have been arguing ever since over the rich legacy of his thought, each faction determined to prove itself his only legitimate heir.

The history of attempts to grapple with the problems of a Marxist theory of ideology can be seen, no doubt simplistically, as a pendulum swinging between the twin Marxist heresies of economism and idealism in search of a position between the two which would not lapse into merely a weak form of either. Economism may be defined as the belief that not only are all social phenomena determined by the economic, but that they are reducible to it. This, by the more refined, is sometimes referred to as vulgar Marxism. By contrast, idealism may be defined in the present context as the belief that ideology is an autonomous structure which ultimately escapes economic determination.

Given the passions aroused by this controversy it is not surprising that Althusser should have been cast by some in the role of fifth columnist of the idealists and by others in the role of Stalinist heavy. Yet it is possible to view his theory as an attempt at a delicate balancing act between these two poles, as an argument for the *relative* autonomy of ideology, which never escapes determination yet is only determined in the last instance; and, as we are told, 'From the first moment to the last, the lonely hour of the "last instance" never comes.'[3] But this center could not hold, and in the wake of the post-Althusserian reaction there has been a perceptible movement back—both towards economism (seen by its supporters as a return to first principles) and towards idealism (seen as a necessary movement beyond the constricting bonds of the Marxist problematic). This latter tendency has been fueled, though whether with his blessing or not is unclear to me, by the historical studies of Michel Foucault, as well as, no doubt, by deep-seated shifts in the political, and ultimately the economic, climate.[4] I anticipate some further steps in this direction. However, taking a lesson from some campaigns of the past, I do not propose to fight on two fronts at once, but will instead confine myself to considering attempts at establishing a more direct relationship between economics and ideology. Even here, given the spatial limitations, only brief skirmishes will be possible.

Is it possible to establish such a relationship without slipping back into reductionism? Within film history there has been a reluctance to deal with the issue, though more recently there has been a growth of interest in the economic history of Hollywood. In a series of papers, Douglas Gomery has undertaken to produce and interrogate basic empirical evidence on the corporate history of the Hollywood majors, and he and others have greatly added to our knowledge of key moments in cinema history such as the introduction of new technologies. Economic history is certainly not inherently reductionist. The magisterial work of Lucien Febvre and Henri-Jean Martin, *The Coming of the Book*, is a history of printing and the book trade which does not claim to be a history of literature.[5] Recently, however, Gomery has proposed that 'we should reexamine all those analyses of film and ideology of the 1930s which employ finance capital as the key link between the economic base and the ideological superstructure.' He suggests we should find this key link in 'the behavior of the monopolistic corporation and the effect of the state,' that effect being, he argues, to reinforce the dominant position of the majors within the industry.[6] Gomery's argument is therefore that the ideology of media production is dictated by the fact that the media are owned by monopoly capital.

Gomery has largely been ploughing a lonely furrow in the United States, but in Britain similar positions have been advanced, albeit in relation to television, which, for a variety of reasons, has been the site of the most interesting theoretical debates on the issue of economic determinacy. Thus Graham Murdock and Peter Golding have argued that concentration and textual study of the media have produced, in effect, a kind of idealist distortion and that:

> the ways in which the mass media function as 'ideological apparatuses' can only be adequately understood when they are systematically related to their position as large-scale commercial enterprises in a capitalist economic system and if these relations are examined historically.[7]

Put thus generally, of course, the proposition is one which must command the assent not only of Marxists of all descriptions, but of any rational person. Who would deny that in order to understand the movies or television we need to take into account the fact that they are produced by large capitalist organizations? But Gomery, Murdock and Golding assert more than this: not merely that there is a connection between economics and ideology, or even that economics is ultimately determining, but that media production and its ideology is *directly* determined by the fact that the means of production are owned by monopoly capitalists. In so doing they are in some danger of being more royalist than the king. Marx' own notion of ideology has been succinctly and precisely formulated by G.A. Cohen: 'the character of the leading ideas of society is explained by their propensity, in virtue of that character, to sustain the structure of economic roles called for by the productive forces.'[8] In other words, ideology is as it is because the economy needs a certain class structure to sustain itself, and this class structure needs in turn a certain ideology to support it. But it is the class structure of society as a whole which requires this certain ideology, not the capitalists who own the film industry. True, their long-term interests, which require that their right of ownership of the means of production be protected, include the maintenance of existing economic roles. But these interests are secured by the ideology which supports society as a whole and which therefore cannot be exclusively limited to the legitimation supplied by films or television programs. The theory that the nature of media products may be explained by the interests of the owners demanding the ideological support of their products actually short-circuits classical Marxist theory.

That, of course, does not invalidate it as a theory. But Terry Lovell has recently pointed out some weaknesses in the formulation. In the first place, while the long-term interests of capital might require the production of films and television programs supportive of capitalist society as a whole in order to secure the property rights of the owners of the media, the short-term interests of the latter might pull them in a different direction:

> If surplus value can be extracted from the production of cultural commodities which challenge, or even subvert, the dominant ideology, then all other things being equal it is in the interests of particular capitals to invest in the production of such commodities.[9]

Lovell's argument here is strictly Marxist, asserting that the question of ownership needs to take into account the concept of contradiction, according to which there may be different interests at work within the economic base, which is, as Raymond Williams has said, 'itself a dynamic and internally contradictory process.'[10] Thus there may be different fractions of capital which can produce contradictions between the ideological needs of the economic system as a whole and the economic interests of some capitalists.

Following this logic, capitalist publishers have made profits from selling the works of Marx.

Such an objection does not invalidate the theory that ownership involves ideological control. It simply states that this control may be exercised in the direction of immediate rather than long-term interest. What is more damaging, perhaps, is Lovell's further point that the theory which argues from ownership, apparently the purest Marxism, takes no account of a further distinction within Marxist theory—that between exchange-value and use-value. The fact that films and television programs circulate as commodities within a capitalist economic system entails no certainty that they will operate in the ideological interests of those who secure the economic benefit:

> there is no guarantee that the use-value of the cultural object for its purchaser will be even compatible with its utility to capitalism as bourgeois ideology, and therefore no guarantee that it will in fact secure 'the ideological effect.'[11]

So even if it were the case that capitalists needed, in order to maintain their legitimacy, to produce products supportive of their position in society, they could not be sure of doing so.

One may indeed press Lovell's point further. In arguing against the current emphasis on textual analysis (an argument, I hasten to add, Gomery has never made) Murdock and Golding have claimed: 'To focus on texts as ideology is to remain blind to the forces which lie behind the production of these texts.'[12] But this claim masks the inability of those who argue from ownership to demonstrate the precise ways in which the economic structure of media industries actually produces specific instances of ideology. I know of no analysis of a film or television program which has explained satisfactorily how every textual effect can be traced to the operation of an immediate economic determinant. Even in texts (granted that there are at least some) whose use-value seems pretty much supportive of capitalist ideology, there is always some surplus, some excess, which resists the attempt to reduce it to a mere rationale for the economic interests of its owners.

But it is important to be clear that this objection does not dispose of the principle of economic determinacy, though at times Lovell seems to want to do so. For while we may admit that within cultural production there are indeed contradictions, the importance we attach to them is a test of the extent to which we are prepared to accept the Marxist claim that ideology is necessary to secure the reproduction of the class system. If we judge that the contradictions are not merely potentially or occasionally but actually and frequently subversive, then the ideological hegemony of the bourgeoisie cannot continue to hold. It is one thing to argue that the system is a leaky vessel, quite another to find that it does not hold water at all.

Nor is it simply a matter of the coherence of the theory. There is also the empirical evidence. Take the case of Hollywood in the 1930s (but contemporary television would do as well). Even if it be granted that in theory the ownership of Hollywood by monopoly capital could, by virtue of contradictions within the economic base, have led to the production of films which did not support capitalism, and even if it also be granted that in any case capitalism cannot guarantee the use-value of its products in its own interests, one would still need to ask: Where are all the films which actually do subvert capitalist ideology? Just as it is difficult to demonstrate exactly how the economic determines the text, so it might be argued that it is difficult to point to large numbers of 'subversive' films. Yet such an argument from empirical evidence is not as forceful as it may appear, since it depends on a reading of the ideology of Hollywood films which is asserted rather than proved. This is an issue to which we shall need to return; let us at this point raise a single question. Suppose for the sake of argument that scarcely any Hollywood films of the 1930s were actively hostile to capitalism in a direct political sense. One could nevertheless make a case for saying that Hollywood was in certain ways strongly subversive of the dominant sexual ideology. How else can one explain the outrage of groups such as the League of Decency and Hollywood's attempts to censor itself through the adoption of the Motion Picture Production Code? No smoke without fire, surely.

Nevertheless, there are still important arguments to be presented in favor of the principle of economic determinacy. Lovell's points about contradiction within the base and the difficulty of guaranteeing use-value take insufficient account both of the complexity of the Marxist position and of what is actually known about the production and consumption of films. In a key passage Marx states that it is 'social being' that determines 'consciousness.'[13] Thus it follows that cultural production is not determined solely by the operation of immediate economic effects but also by the ways in which the people who work in the industry are themselves 'produced.' Their consciousness is produced in part by their social being within the professional world they inhabit. And we can only understand why films are the way they are if we look not merely at who owns the means of production but also at the real material conditions under which they are produced. Unfortunately we do not know as much about this as we ought, and perhaps what we do know— because that knowledge has often been produced by the more empirically-minded—has not always been absorbed into theory.

It might indeed be in the interests of the owners to produce profitable films which subvert capitalist ideology, but films are made by professional filmmakers, not by the owners of the means of production. There is at least a strong probability that recruitment into the industry will be governed by ideological predispositions built into social institutions which themselves support the class structure. For example, in a study contemporary with the phenomenon, Leo Rosten states that at the end of the 1930s only a tiny proportion of 'creative' workers originated from the working class.[14] And in an important study of the role of the banks in Hollywood, Janet Wasko has found that with the structure of financial control as it existed in the 1930s, 'close scrunity proved unnecessary as management positions could be filled by those with the same goals as the banks, and these managers would adhere to policies set by owners and lenders.' If one were looking for films that are in some sense 'subversive' one might expect to find more of them in the so-called 'independent' sector of production. But Wasko further argues that independent producers were not necessarily more free:

> . . . the independent producer encountered various restrictions and limitations from bankers throughout the production and distribution process. As *Fortune* noted in 1949: 'The banker develops a protective skein of infinite detail, every contract is examined, every expenditure governed. He does not positively tell the producer how to write the script, but he does tell him what to leave out.'[15]

In passing one may note that a great deal of writing about film history does in fact make use of this notion of the materiality of cultural practices. Thus Gerald Mast describes the studio system in the 1930s in terms of a set of relatively rigid working methods tending towards the enforcement of uniformity (and attributable ultimately to economic forces):

> The studio system was as pervasive in erasing stylistic differences as it was in blurring differences of theme and story. The director not only inherited a detailed scenario that he could not alter but a completed series of sets and costumes and a studio crew of cameramen, electricians, and soundmen. Any director's impulses toward personal style were suppressed before shooting began by the studio's general policies of lighting, design, cinematography, and cutting.[16]

(The difference between this and a Marxist theory of cultural production, however, is that such a formulation tends to conceive of the production process as a set of real, concrete restraints on another category, the director's 'creativity,' which escapes a materialist analysis.)

The contention here, as against Lovell, is that the actual process of production is itself penetrated by economic forces, sometimes directly and sometimes mediated through the effects of other social institutions on the consciousness of filmmakers. This militates against the possibility of 'subversive' work being produced. But it is equally important to recognize the extent to which capital has penetrated the process of consumption. Even if Hollywood could not *guarantee* the use-value of its films, large resources were devoted to influencing the ways in which films were consumed. The apparatus of publicity departments and the careful orchestration of the exhibition of films (design of theaters, 'showmanship' and so on) ensured that audiences were not simply left to make up their own minds about how to 'read' a film.

Yet if we accept the force of these arguments, we can find ourselves pushed almost irresistibly back into reductionism. The problem is still how to hold on to the notion of economic determinacy (without which we are no longer talking about Marxism at all—which may not worry some of us; but then one has to ask what other explanations, properly speaking, are on offer which are not ultimately mere descriptions or, to use Bloch's phrase, enumerations) while doing justice to the complexity of the cinematic institution. It is this difficulty which has prompted some British Marxists to refine the central metaphor of base and superstructure, a metaphor as productive of confusions as it is of insights. Thus Raymond Williams has tried to shift the meaning of 'determination,' the concept governing the operation of the base on the superstructure, away from signifying fixed and rigid 'laws' and towards a notion of the economic 'setting limits' and exerting 'pressure.'[17] In some ways this is helpful. The role of economics within the industry (ownership, financial pressures) remains important in that it defines the space within which texts are produced. Economics would contribute much to answering such questions as why Hollywood was wholly given over to the production of entertainment, to feature films of a certain length, type, and so forth (whereas television, certainly in Britain, was not). But if we confine the role of economics to that of setting limits and exerting pressures, then we are still left without an explanation of that which exists within the limits or that on which pressure is exerted. Ideology comes to be seen as something which is always distinct from economics. Instead of being the economic in another form or, to paraphrase Clausewitz, the continuation of the economic by other means, ideology is seen as quite discrete. What Williams' model cannot then adequately account for is where ideology comes from.

And so while the role of the economic structure of Hollywood in the 1930s can be seen in terms of defining a space for operations of ideology, this does not dispose of the role which economics plays in the production of that ideology in specific films. What the role is can, of course, only be understood as a result of careful investigation. But my assumption would be that it is not unconnected to the fact, for example, that Franklin D. Roosevelt, who, despite contemporary assertions to the contrary, was not an anti-capitalist, was between 1932 and 1944 four times elected to the Presidency. This fact in its turn must have been related to the need of the economic system as a whole, to ensure that even in a time of great stress a political ideology favorable to capitalism was maintained—as indeed it was. We are not dealing here with mere coincidences, surely.

The difficulties of teasing out such relationships in any particular instance are daunting. All the same, one must try. History, after all, is not philosophy, not just about theoretical relations but actual cases. *Our Daily Bread*, directed by King Vidor in 1934 and distributed by United Artists, throws some interesting light on the problem. To begin with, the sheer difficulties of getting the film made seem to demonstrate the force of the argument that the question of ownership is the key. The story of the film concerns the efforts of a group of unemployed people to establish a farm co-operative. Vidor, who up to this time had worked most frequently for MGM, took the project to Irving Thalberg, who was 'intrigued by the possibilities,' according to Vidor, but 'didn't think it was an appropriate subject for MGM.'[18] Vidor then took his idea to other studios, which again 'seemed intrigued by the story and enthusiastic about the project, but all the major companies were afraid to make a film without glamor, even though admitting that the struggle depicted was a heroic one.'[19] Finally, Vidor went to see his friend Charlie Chaplin, a part-owner of United Artists, who promised that his company would release the film. Vidor then approached the banks for production finance, but with no success. As he recounts in his autobiography:

> When a banker reads a script in which a bank forces a sheriff to make a foreclosure sale which a disreputable-looking group of neighbors won't permit, he doesn't feel kindly toward your venture. Nor, as I learned at first-hand, does he mince words in refusing to lend you the money to make the film.[20]

Vidor finally raised some money by mortgaging his house.

One of the difficulties in proving that the structure of ownership in the film industry does have effects on production is that, in a sense, the case depends on all the films that don't get made. *Our Daily Bread* is the next best thing, a film which very nearly did not get made. Yet one could equally well see the film as making a case for Lovell's argument that the search for immediate profit can lead to the production of films contrary to the ideological interests of their owners. Chaplin chose to back it because it offered the prospect of profits for his company. (One need not read very far into Chaplin's own autobiography to get the impression that his sympathy for progressive ideas was unlikely to seduce him into unprofitable business ventures. On the other hand, if one takes a less cynical view, one might see the existence of someone like Chaplin as evidence that the system did allow for recruitment from outside the supporters of the dominant order; and after all, there is plenty of evidence elsewhere that it did, up to a point—the point, perhaps, where they were able to put their ideas into practice, since for every mogul like Chaplin there were dozens who lacked the real power to have any effect.)

But to discuss the film in these terms is already to prejudice the issue of whether *Our Daily Bread* actually challenges capitalist ideology. Contemporary reviews only demonstrate the varying possibilities of its reception. *Motion Picture Herald* saw the film less as an exploration of new social models than as a comment on the weather:

> For topical subject matter it would be difficult to find a theme more pertinent currently or more widely applicable than the drought which has paralyzed and withered farm produce and small city business of the Northwest, Middlewest and Southwest.[21]

Picturegoer thought it was about 'the "back to the land" movement.'[22] *Kinematograph Weekly* agreed: 'Back to Nature as a solution to one of the many urgent economic problems of today.'[23] According to Vidor the Hearst press called the film 'pinko,' while the Russians would award it only second prize at the Moscow film festival because it was 'capitalistic propaganda.'[24] Subsequently Andrew Bergman has viewed the film as not directly political at all: 'Vidor was concerned with life styles rather than economics, with cooperation as a way people related to each other rather than as a solution to the Depression.'[25] Raymond Durgnat, in the most subtle attempt so far at teasing out the film's ideological position, argues that the cooperativism which the film presents is nearer to primitive capitalism than to communism in that it ignores the latter's emphasis on economic planning:

> *Our Daily Bread*'s dramatic structure hinges on the co-operative producing an abundant corn crop during the Depression, a period of catastrophic under-demand during which farmers were notoriously burning the very crop which Vidor's co-operative was laboring so heroically to produce.[26]

Yet there are other interpretations possible. The economics of producing corn during the Depression are only viewable as primitive capitalism if one accepts the presuppositions of capitalist economics. Only if corn production is seen as production for exchange-value is it pointless. But if capitalism has resulted in a collapse of the exchange value of corn, it still has a use-value. People can eat it.

Any assessment of the ideological effect of *Our Daily Bread* in 1934 would also need to take into account the number of people to whom that effect became available. But here again we are faced with uncertainties. Lewis Jacobs states that the film was a 'box office failure.'[27] An exhibitor in Idaho described it as 'a flop.'[28] Vidor says it didn't do badly,[29] and some facts seem to bear him out: it took $18,000 at the Rialto in New York in its first week, as against the previous year's high of $32,000 for *The Lost Patrol* and a low of $5,800 for *Destination Unknown/The Fighting President*;[30] it was down to $10,000 in the second week and then ended its run.[31]

So what may we conclude? Certainly not that ownership of the industry by monopoly capitalism is the key link between the economic base and the ideological superstructure in the Hollywood of the 1930s. True, the case of *Our Daily Bread* certainly demonstrates that the owners of the industry exerted pressure (although even here the argument is perhaps not conclusive since Vidor's comments suggest that MGM turned it down less because of its anti-capitalism than because the project didn't conform to MGM's brand of high-gloss entertainment). However, the film's (indeed any film's) ideological complexity demands a more 'over-determined' explanation. But such an explanation does not thereby escape economics. Thus, to take our example, I do not see how *Our Daily Bread* can be understood without reference to populism, whether we conceive of it as a purely reactionary political philosophy or agree with Ernesto Laclau that 'there is no socialism without populism.'[32] And there is at least a *prima facie* case for saying that the populism of 1930s America was determined by the ideological needs of the economic system, albeit in complex ways. Economic determinants are still there, but they are not to be confined to those operating upon the industry directly.

It is of course the very 'complexity' of the question which encourages some to seek for simple and rigid 'laws,' while others take refuge in what they see as the unavoidable imprecision of the historical enterprise, whose concepts are inevitably inadequate to encompass the myriad reality they must describe. Thus Edward Thompson in *The Poverty of Theory* writes:

> Historical concepts and rules are often of this order. They display extreme elasticity and allow for great irregularity; the historian appears to be evading rigour as he disappears into the largest generalizations at one moment, while at the next moment he disappears into the particularities of the qualifications in any special case. This provokes distrust, and even laughter, within other disciplines. Historical materialism employs concepts of equal generality and elasticity—'exploitation,' 'hegemony,' 'class struggle'—and as expectations rather than as rules. And even categories which appeal to offer less elasticity—'feudalism,' 'capitalism,' 'the bourgeoisie'—appear in historical practice, not as ideal types fulfilled in historical evolution, but as whole families of special cases, families which include adopted orphans and the children of typological miscegenation. History knows no regular verbs.[33]

To this Perry Anderson has replied, in words I cannot better, that Thompson gives too much away:

His argument in effect amounts to a claim for a legitimate laxity of notions that would be the peculiar privilege of the historian. But the nature of the historical process warrants no such special licence. The fact that its object continually changes no more relieves the discipline of history of the duty of formulating clear and exact concepts for its comprehension than it does meteorology—a physical science whose data notoriously change rather more swiftly and mercurially than those of history itself. If the weather remains largely unpredictable (and uncontrollable), the meteorologist does not resign himself to professions of the inherent approximation of his study: he seeks to push back the limits of our knowledge by further scientific investigation, which will involve not less but more conceptualization, of wider ranges of evidence. So it is in every other science. History is no exception. Brecht once remarked that if human behaviour appears unpredictable, it is not because there are no determinations, but because there are too many.[34]

What this suggests for film history is neither that we abandon the concepts we have, on the grounds that the facts are too complicated, nor that we assume that they have already answered our problems. To say that economics determines ideology is at once obvious and useless. The question is, how precisely? To answer it we need both more theory (adequate, for example, to do more than tell us that a certain film is 'capitalist ideology') and more evidence (I am sure that more could be discovered about why the studios turned down Our Daily Bread; I have not been able to go beyond secondary sources). And we shall always need more, because the relationships we are attempting to describe are not fixed but changing. What was true of Hollywood in the 1930s is not necessarily true today. No doubt it is an economic determination upon scholars that they are always calling for more research. Like anyone else we have children to support. Nevertheless it is the case that, in the words of Marc Bloch, 'in history, as elsewhere, the causes cannot be assumed. They are to be looked for. . . .'[35]

NOTES

1. Marc Bloch, *The Historian's Craft* (New York: Vintage Books, 1953), p. 10.

2. Colin MacCabe, 'Realism and the Cinema: Notes on Some Brechtian Theses,' *Screen*, vol. 15, no. 2 (1974), pp. 22-23.

3. Louis Althusser, *For Marx* (Harmondsworth: Penguin, 1969), p. 113.

4. For two points of view on Foucault's attitude toward Marxism, see the correspondence between Colin Gordon and Alan Sheridan in the *Times Literary Supplement* during May, 1981, following Gordon's review of Sheridan's book, *Michel Foucault: The Will to Truth*.

5. Lucien Febvre and Henri-Jean Martin, *The Coming of the Book: The Impact of Printing 1450-1800*, trans. David Gerard, ed. Geoffrey Nowell-Smith and David Wootton (London: New Left Books, 1976).

6. Douglas Gomery, 'Rethinking US Film History: The Depression Decade and Monopoly Control,' *Film and History*, vol. 10, no. 2 (1980), p. 37.

7. Graham Murdock and Peter Golding, 'Ideology and the Mass Media: The Question of Determination,' in *Ideology and Cultural Production*, ed. Michèle Barrett *et al.* (London: Croom Helm, 1979), pp. 204-205.

8. G.A. Cohen, *Karl Marx's Theory of History* (Oxford: Oxford University Press, 1978), p. 279.

9. Terry Lovell, *Pictures of Reality* (London: British Film Institute, 1980), p. 61.

10. Raymond Williams, *Marxism and Literature* (Oxford: Oxford University Press, 1977), p. 82.

11. Lovell, p. 60.

12. Murdock and Golding, p. 220.

13. In the often cited Preface to *A Contribution to the Critique of Political Economy*, ed. Maurice Dobb (Woodstock, NY: Beekman Publishers, 1972).

14. Leo Rosten, *Hollywood: The Movie Colony, The Movie Makers* (1941; rpt. New York: Arno Press, 1970), pp. 387f.

15. Janet Wasko, 'Relationships between the American Motion Picture Industry and Banking Institutions' (Ph.D. Dissertation, University of Illinois, 1980), pp. 130, 162.

16. Gerald Mast, *A Short History of the Movies* (Indianapolis, IN: Bobbs-Merrill, 1976), p. 268.

17. Williams, pp. 85, 87.

18. King Vidor, *A Tree is a Tree* (New York: Harcourt, Brace & Co., 1953), pp. 221.

19. Ibid., p. 222.

20. Ibid., p. 223.

21. *Motion Picture Herald*, 18 August 1934.

22. *Picturegoer*, 6 July 1935.

23. *Kinematograph Weekly*, 3 January 1935.

24. Vidor, p. 226.

25. Andrew Bergman, *We're in the Money* (New York: Harper & Row, 1972), p. 79.

26. Raymond Durgnat, 'King Vidor,' *Film Comment*, vol. 9, no. 4 (1973), p. 32.

27. Lewis Jacobs, *The Rise of the American Film* (New York: Teachers College Press, 1968), p. 458.

28. *Motion Picture Herald*, 16 February 1935.

29. Vidor, p. 226.

30. *Motion Picture Herald*, 13 October 1934.

31. *Motion Picture Herald*, 20 October 1934.

32. Ernesto Laclau, *Politics and Ideology in Marxist Theory* (London: New Left Books, 1977), p. 196.

33. Edward P. Thompson, *The Poverty of Theory* (London: Merlin Press, 1978), p. 238.

34. Perry Anderson, *Arguments Within English Marxism* (London: Verso Editions, 1980), p. 10.

35. Bloch, p. 197.

Securing the Historical:
Historiography and the Classical Cinema

Philip Rosen

1

For some time it has been a commonplace that writing histories of the cinema has been made difficult by empirical problems of ascertaining just what went on. However, as we begin to learn more about what did go on, it appears that at least as problematic is the conceptualization of what it should be to write histories of the cinema. In my view conceptualizing *cinema* history is inseparable from conceptualizing history more generally.

In this regard, and even at what some of us might wish to regard as this late date, it is not clear that we have surpassed discussions of the historical as conceived in certain centers of Western theoretical debate during the late 19th and early 20th centuries. In our own time Marx, Nietzsche, Saussure and Freud have served as acknowledged origins of much advanced theoretical discourse. Thus we should not be too surprised if one of the crucial epistemological issues of their time, namely the nature and possibility of historical knowledge, returns. And neither will it be surprising that newer concepts useful for thinking through the work of the historian—ideological practice, interpellation, the Imaginary—are direct products or developments of products from this period.[1]

For a privileged example, briefly consider one of the most obvious arenas of controversy among practicing historians, that of historical explanation. Insofar as historiography is ideological practice and implies ideological struggle, explanation is one of the most significant sites of that struggle, and the nature of that struggle is of some interest. If historiographic discourse is considered as a form of consciousness, then explanation can be considered as the explicit freezing of that discourse into fixed consciousness, a positionality of meaning, the meaning of history. On this view, explanation is the point where the historian can stop. Mastery of the past—or at least one version of it—has been proposed.

In this sense, explanation is an Imaginary component of the historian's semiotic activity. The social role of historical explanation might be understood through this formulation. Such an understanding would require an attention to the forms of coherence and verisimilitude in historiography.[2] Then it would be possible to assert that when we distinguish among forms of historical explanation, we are distinguishing among forms of a historiographic Imaginary and, simultaneously, among forms of ideological interpellation.

Considering history in terms of theories of textuality makes it possible to link the analysis of historiography to that of other discursive domains. In addition, it foregrounds the problem of conceiving of the Imaginary as part of the network of historical determinations: no society without ideology, no discourse without some form of the Imaginary, no historiography outside subjective positions. One of the great lessons of psychoanalytic feminist film theory seems to me to be the centrality of comprehending the possibility and significance of variations in the Imaginary component of discourse. Whereas ten or fifteen years ago it perhaps seemed possible to some to equate the Symbolic with contradiction and, therefore, ideological demystification with the revelation of the Symbolic function, it has rapidly become evident that a key political matter, and hence historical problem, has to do with the imbrication of the Imaginary with the Symbolic. Here, this perspective will refer us to the question of position—textual, historiographic and historical.

The Imaginary function of historiography, then, is itself a large problem in the conceptualization of history and for the historiography that follows from such a conceptualization. Recent film history and criticism have been exemplary in their interrogation of the mechanisms of the Imaginary in cinema as grounds for the ideological interpellations which cinema supplies to society. For this reason cinema may provide an interesting site for an exploration of the general questions involved in conceptualizing history as well as the history of images and sounds. This is the context for the points, many of them speculative, which follow.

2

A few years ago, during a discussion of the notion of popular memory, Stephen Heath tied together a number of themes from the psychoanalytic investigation of cinematic interpellation, such as the imaginary signifier, family romance and the filmic *histoire*. He described the presentation of history in classical cinema as follows:

> No historical film—in the everyday sense of a film aiming to deal with some past period or event—escapes fiction: the fiction of the cinematic apparatus, the imaginary signifier, but also, quite simply, the fiction of presenting the past, which in turn is the obligation of an ordering, a narration, a historical discourse. In the classic cinema, family romance is there as the point of such a discourse—at once in the specific sense that the historical film engages exactly the novel of noble lives, heroes, famous figures, and, more importantly, in the wider sense that the constant force of the narrative of history given is familiar and family history: individuals, lives, passions, mothers, fathers, brothers, sisters, sons, daughters, the whole panoply of domestic conflicts. History is shut into that order, provided with the perfection of a story ('a closed discourse with both a finality and an end' [—Greimas]). The story orders the film, patterns, identifications, defines a movement and a continuity, holding the spectator to them for completion and the illusion of 'truth.' Which illusion is a constitutive tourniquet: film is like history, absent in the representation, in the past presented; history is like a film, another genre but the same narrative patterns, the same familiarity, without problem or division.[3]

Here classical cinematic narrative is treated as an *histoire* like history to demonstrate a coincidence between narrative patternings which appeal to a spectator in two interlinked discourses—familial *and* historical, individual *and* social. The actual presence of history itself is impossible, but a secure historical truth is nevertheless experienced. Heath's description provides an introduction for certain considerations.

Recently, certain theorists have thought it useful to note that the period which gave rise to cinema is that which gave rise to psychoanalysis. Here we might note another coincidence: this same period marks an extreme, if locally varied, tension in Western historiographic thought. Shifts in that thinking, sometimes experienced as crises of knowledge, occurred. On the heels of Hegel, Marx and positivism, the second half of the 19th century saw the development of a number of problematics which questioned the security of historical knowledge or at least changed conceptions of that knowledge.

The standard accounts of historiography in Germany and the United States during this period provide examples of the nature of this shift. Germany's was perhaps the most influential historiographic culture of modern times. At the end of the century, official thought seemed secure and optimistic. However, as positivism was confronted by neo-Kantianism, German intellectuals encountered the so-called crisis of historicism, the nature of which crisis can be indicated by names such as Rickert, Dilthey,

Weber, and (slightly later) Mannheim. To some of the most outstanding theorists of the period, the weakening of epistemological security which resulted from the radical questioning of historical knowledge could only be met by an appeal to Marxism. The younger Lukács is exemplary here. Others, as different as Dilthey and Weber, could only face these questions as inevitable and tragic. Georg C. Iggers has summed up the standard view of German historiography during the period when analysts of culture were first compelled to confront Freud, Jung, Nietzsche, Dilthey and Bergson, as well as Baudelaire, Dostoevsky and Proust:

> The historians and social scientists increasingly forsook their occupation with the problem of what constituted society and history; instead they asked how a science of history or society was possible. They tended to regard all knowledge, which went beyond constructions based upon empirical data, [sic] as colored by human subjectivity. The solution of any ultimate problems became impossible; the gulf between the world of Being and the world of Meaning apparently was complete. The collapse of the Newtonian picture of the physical universe, at the turn of the century, and the construction of non-Euclidean systems of geometries further seemed to stress the limitations of human knowledge. Any interpretation of reality, other than one based upon strict induction, was doomed as poetry or imagination. The reliance upon empirical data alone, it was felt, would reveal a universe basically without meaning.[4]

The form of the historiographic shift in the United States seems to elicit a different kind of description. As one might expect, instead of a tortured idealist critique of the conditions of the possibility of thought, the dominant new current in the writing of history partook of positivism. Nevertheless, an interesting change is discernible, one which is evident not only in the production of historiography but also in the mechanisms of its sociocultural reception.

The impact of the German university on American intellectual life of the late 19th century has often been noted. Indeed, the roots of our current system of graduate study and degrees lie to a great extent in the steady trickle of young Americans who studied in Germany during this period. More specifically, the 1890s mark the end of the domination of American historiography by self-financed gentlemen-scholars of broad education but little formal training. The end of this era, during which the work of such gentlemen had marked the writing of history as a rich man's (sic) activity, can be located by the deaths of George Bancroft in 1891 and Francis Parkman in 1893. Richard Hofstadter summarizes the transition that occurred thus:

> [T]he development of the modern American university, which went on with breathtaking rapidity in the years after 1870, brought into being a

whole new class of historians, the academic professionals. In the last two decades of the nineteenth century there took place a rapid transformation of the prevailing model of historical work. A discipline that had once been dominated by well-to-do gentlemen-amateurs inspired by a literary ideal and writing grand narrative history aimed at (if not always successfully reaching) a broad reading public was now rather rapidly taken over by professional scholars, recruited to a striking degree from the middle and lower middle classes, academically trained and academically employed, inspired by the scientific ideal, and writing for the most part highly focused monographic inquiries intended for other professionals.[5]

One result, according to Hofstadter, was a displacement of the mythic appeal of historiography, based partly on the changes in the dominant forms of what the culture treated as sophisticated writing of history. Unlike the large-scale narrative histories of nations, which carried their own general significance *in the telling* of the story of the country, the monograph was to be only a contribution to the achievement of a large truth which could be formulated *outside* the specific historiographic work itself—the large-scale hypothesis which a monograph tested. Interestingly, the best-known of that first generation of historians produced by the flowering of American graduate schools in history—famous examples are Frederick Jackson Turner and Charles Beard—were the ones who produced hypotheses of such sweep that debates about the role of the frontier in American development or the economic motives of the founding fathers extended far beyond the profession. This kind of ideological appeal was something the monographs themselves apparently could not supply. There had to be general significance to make sense of the particular case studies. Some of those who supplied such hypotheses might become famous, but they were few. In summary, it is reasonable to suggest that there was a shift in the institutionalized forms of American historiography, hence in the kind of ideological address it was enacting and in its sociocultural functioning during this period.

As comparative cases in social and intellectual history, American and German historiography must, of course, be differentiated. In Germany, the strong speculative philosophical tradition forced working historians to confront theoretical difficulties earlier than in the United States. Also, in the United States the university was already becoming a location of upward mobility in status if not always in class. Nevertheless, the avant-garde American philosophy of the period certainly had its own relativistic implications (William James was well known in Europe during his own lifetime). It was not long before positivist confidence was challenged by the ethical and epistemological insecurity towards which so many advanced European philosophical and historical theories led. By the time of the Great

Depression, even Beard was arguing that Americans could not escape those unfortunate problems that Europeans had already been confronting for thirty years.

3

Thus the appearance of the machine for ideal looking, cinema, was coincident with a crisis in the security of history's meaning and knowledge. One of the striking things about cinema, of course, is the early and (to this point) permanent way the dominant, naturalized versions of it seem to have been channeled into narrative. The dominant cinema is narrative cinema, and the dominant look it provides thus supports and is supported by a position of narrative knowledge, as a number of writers have been arguing for some time now.[6] Heath points out certain similarities between the so-called classical cinema, with its so-called classical narrative construction, and certain kinds of historiographic discourse, undoubtedly those which Hofstadter associated with the American gentlemen-scholars of the 19th century. The French play on the word *histoire* in narrative analysis thus does seem to point to something significant in the present context. As we explore the question of the historiographic Imaginary and the history of cinema, then, it may therefore be of use to consider the presentation of history *in* classical cinema.

This can begin from an impression. Generally speaking, it seems that the historical was integrated into classical cinema as a topic quite rapidly. The dominant cinema appears to have appropriated the presentation of the overtly historical past as one significant (not to mention profitable) task fairly early. And this presentation was not simple reenactment, a kind of pseudo-documentary, but rather gave events significance, demonstrated meaning immanent in the history it carried. Yet, meaning discoverable as immanent in history was exactly what was challenged by the shifts in historiography contemporaneous with the appearance of cinema. That is, what is striking is the way the historical as meaning-full was so quickly integrated into and made important for cinema at this particular historical moment.

Paradigmatic examples could be made of what so many ideological discourses tell us mark the origins and limits of classical cinema: *Birth of a Nation* and *Intolerance*. It is possible to collect elements from several accounts of these films to arrive at the following synthesis: the classical cinema has a genius father (Griffith), a first-born (*Birth of a Nation*), and a magnificent freak (*Intolerance*). The father wishes to be the historian for the masses and bring them the truth about the past. Thus, at the birth of cinema as 'art,' he presents the masses with the event which was the obsessive trauma of American politics and historiography of his generation: the Civil War.

Given this kind of evidently effective account of *Birth of a Nation*, it is worthwhile to briefly consider certain aspects of the film. As spectators, assured by the secure look offered by cinema, we observe characters typical of various historical forces of their time. But despite that general significance, these characters also possess a certain minimum of individual traits which motivate their movements through a family romance plot in which individual destinies remain of concern. Thus, we observe individual characters living on the margins of great events, but we are also to understand them as representing historically typical situations. Therefore we can comprehend great motive 'truths' of history which transcend individual destinies. (A famous example of such a motive truth for the film is the importance of race.) Such truths can be or may become evident to the characters through their experiences as individuals; or the characters can be propelled by such truths without being aware of them; and those truths can be bluntly and directly given to the audience through intertitles (some of which attest to the historical authenticity of specific images and general narrative meaning by means of footnote-like citations of preexisting texts) or even visual allegory, such as the Christian imagery which concludes the film.

From this conclusion of *Birth of a Nation* it is not far to *Intolerance*, where the general truths often take over as virtual abstractions; the most famous example of such an abstraction in a visual presentation is the repeated image of Lillian Gish as the mother rocking the cradle, but the intercutting of the four stories can easily be analyzed in these terms. The consequences of Griffith's explorations into an intellectual cinema for a middle-class culture are often seen as troubling for American film history or even disastrous for the 'father of film art.' For example, in his once standard survey of world cinema history, Arthur Knight barely touches on Griffith's career after *Birth of a Nation*, and there has been a strong tendency among film historians to treat *Intolerance* as an experimental peak and/or the beginning of a decline. My point here is not accuracy (it can be argued that the rest of Griffith's career indicates that he learned some kind of lesson from the fate of *Intolerance*, for he went on to make a number of films which could be placed in any pantheon of the mainstream cinema), but symptom. *Intolerance* has often been described as having gone beyond the bounds of classical cinema; in such accounts, Griffith was in 1916 either an experimentalist or a failed narrativist, which failure is variously said to be marked by dissipated narrative line, character overcome by theme, theme overcome by form, and/or lost audience.[7]

But let us keep in mind that mythical origin of classical cinema, *Birth of a Nation*. The methods of narrative organization of that film involve a balance, evidently not held in *Intolerance*, between individual motives and traits on the one hand and general truths on the other. The balance is achieved through the mediation of family romance situations in historically significant settings. This method remained a staple of classical cinema. There were, in fact, a number of elaborate variations possible within this framework.

One rich instance is the 1939 Warner Brothers film *The Roaring Twenties*. Clearly a gangster genre movie, it has an explicit ideological project of presenting to the American public an explanation of the 1920s as a licentious aberration in American history, a period whose excesses would be surpassed to enable the construction of a good society. The three major male characters meet during a World War I battle. A tripartite character structure establishes George (Humphrey Bogart) as incurably violent, Lloyd (Jeffrey Lynn) as civilized and uncomfortable with violence, and Eddie (James Cagney) as occupying a place between the other two. Eddie will typify a number of the difficulties and confusions the film presents Americans as having experienced after World War I: desiring to work, he cannot find employment; not looking for trouble, he has nevertheless been made excitable and nervous by the war; willing to accept honest work, he is tough enough to employ shady means to get ahead; ultimately wishing to leave the gangster life and settle down with the woman of his dreams, he tries to use the rackets to rise high enough in social class to attain her. With such normal economic and sexual motivations, he allies himself with the violent George. This alliance turns out to be a kind of pact with the devil, presented as characteristic of America during the 20s. At the climax of the film, having lost his love and ruined financially by the twin disasters of the crash of 1929 and the repeal of prohibition, Eddie finally understands his place in the film and thus in history. The sexual line of the plot works him into a climactic situation where he will kill George and be killed himself, but his own understanding of the action is historical. As he tells George before killing him:

> 'It's a new kind of setup you don't understand. Guys don't go around tearin' things apart like we used ta. People try ta build things up, 'n that's what Lloyd's tryin' ta do. In this new setup—you 'n me just don't belong. That's all.'

What makes *The Roaring Twenties* especially interesting here is not just this standard dramatic self-realization, but also the complexity of the film's historiographic address. While the film presents history by and through the typical individual, it also utilizes direct address to the audience. This direct address is in the form of a newsreel-like authoritative voice-over during the no less than nine 'Hollywood montage' sequences interspersed throughout the movie. From the beginning this voice-over is a virtual voice of history. By the end it has proclaimed a historical shift and explanation: it assures the audience that the disorders of the gangster years are now terminated, thanks to the election of Roosevelt and the resulting end of prohibition. The self-congratulatory and self-confirming aspects of this historiography are clear, for these reforms are said by the voice-over to have occurred on the basis of 'a new determination by an aroused public that law and order should once more reign.' Hence, for the film to conclude with the proper general truth, a shift in audience identity appears to have been necessary. Up to this point Eddie/Cagney, undoubtedly the chief object of secondary cinematic identification, has typified the American public. But at the beginning of the narrative segment in which Eddie attains tragic self-awareness, the voice of history displaces Eddie's typicality; Eddie cannot change and therefore will die, but the audience for the film presumably has already changed (after all, both Roosevelt and repeal of prohibition were firmly in place in 1939). The voice-over authorizes a split in the identity of the audience to suggest the possibility of a moral national harmony already accomplished, a future already in operation. (If *Intolerance* is a kind of *October* for a middle-class culture, perhaps *The Roaring Twenties* should be treated as a kind of *Old and New*.)[8]

This rather shrewd variation on the narrative organization of history indicates the importance to those making Hollywood films not just of history, but simultaneously of address. The identity at play in *The Roaring Twenties* is not just that of the individual spectator in relation to the cinematic apparatus and/or to Eddie/Cagney. That identity also has to do with the American public in relation to itself. That is, national identity is at stake in the address of this film. Meaning inseparable from national purpose—a historiographic Imaginary during the 19th century—appears even in this gangster film, and even for the (then) most recent historical period. This may confirm the pervasiveness of certain goals of *Birth of a Nation*, which, though it is not a point of origin, remains a model classical film for a number of historical and analytical reasons. In this context *The Roaring Twenties* demonstrates how aptly named is the Griffith film, how important for classical cinema has been what Fredric Jameson calls 'the great fantasms of the various nationalisms, now themselves virtual "subjects of history". . .'[9]

4

It is sometimes implied that we might want to consider classical cinema as being in a loose sense an Aristotelian cinema, in order to differentiate it from a more disruptive Brechtian cinema. My description of the historiographic investment of classical cinema suggests another name: that Marxist admirer of Aristotle and defender of classical realist novels, Georg Lukács. It might be productive on occasion to associate classical cinema with a Lukácsian aesthetic. The purpose of this is not just to repeat the kind of comparison between classical cinema and the classic realist novel outlined by commentators such as Colin MacCabe.[10] It is rather to come back to my introductory remarks by a somewhat circuitous route: Lukács was deeply involved in the crisis of German historicism, and his early version of Marxism was a direct response to that crisis.

Especially interesting is the fact that Lukács traces the methodological roots of the classic realist novel not just back to Balzac, but to Walter Scott's innovations in the historical novel. For Lukács, the historical forces which led to the historical novel as practiced by Scott were those which led to the rise of Marxism as a political and intellectual force: the needs of various classes in the political and ideological struggles of their period. Further, the two are united by a common epistemological goal, which is a totalizing perspective on history—exactly what appeared impossible by the end of the 19th century and led to the crisis of historicism.

Lukács' analysis of Scott's work is famous. Here it recalls some of my remarks about the classical cinema. According to Lukács, Scott fabricated plots which center on a protagonist caught between two opposing historical forces. That protagonist's personal choices thus spring from historical conflicts, until, in order to resolve them, the plot introduces purer characters exceptionally typical of the opposing historical forces. Thus, the general motive truths of historical processes, including their necessary interrelationship in a meaningful totality, are called forth by the plot just as history itself called them forth.

From Scott's strategy develops the best of the contemporary novel, what Lukács valorized elsewhere as critical realism. On the basis of a position on what historical knowledge is, Lukács thus inserts himself into the theoretical tradition promoting organic unity as the grasp of general truths through mimesis of particular events and individuals, and promotes his own special stress on the construction of exceptionally typical characters which unite particular and general.[11] Lukács' arguments concerning the conjunction of goals of realist narrative and proper historiography can lead to a speculation on and in broad congruities between a Lukácsian aesthetic (as opposed to a Brechtian aesthetic) on the one hand, and an aesthetic of classical cinema (as opposed to modernist cinema) on the other hand.

The simplest point in such a speculation would be to reinforce the hypothesis that, to different degrees, each classical film offers in its ideological interpellation a version of and attitude toward history, whether or not the film is explicitly historical. This is to be felt by the audience through the experience of a character who might or might not understand his or her own situation within the world of the work. The resulting narrative system would obscure issues revolving around the means of constructing that world, just as Lukács notoriously ignores issues of literary language and attacks writers who foreground such issues. Thus, classically (as it were), the Imaginary point of complete knowledge—of the work and thus of the world it represents—cannot confront its own imbrication in the Symbolic. Certainly, at least, this is the charge of those who have attacked this aesthetic with reference to the name of Brecht.

Nevertheless, it must be kept in mind that for a text to obscure issues of its own means and processes of representation is not to eliminate such issues. We are dealing here with idealized tendencies, not formal absolutes, and the Brechtian-Lukácsian antithesis cannot be defined by mutually exclusive formal oppositions to be summarized simply as presence or absence of transparency. Lukács does not propound a naive realism (it was possible for Brecht to charge Lukács with 'Formalism').[12] Similarly, the classical film does not work as an absolutely smooth transparency. Not only is there the problem of genres, preeminently the musical, which seem to involve somewhat different mechanisms than those which would revolve around the concept of transparency. Also, as Heath among others has argued, the economy of fetishistic fascination is never one of simple immersion in mere illusion.[13] Hence, even in a film which presents history, the historiographic Imaginary at work often seems to require some self-conscious manipulation of its own mechanisms so that they are not completely hidden even to a postulated ideal reader or spectator. The footnotes in *Birth of a Nation* and the double interpellation of *The Roaring Twenties*, both of which have to do with non-mimetic address as conveying guaranteed knowledge, can serve as quick examples.

All of this leads to a major point about our model of classical cinema. There has been a tendency in film studies to fix on the look as ensuring knowledge for the spectator, that is, to emphasize the psychic investments in *looking at* (though also, occasionally, *listening to*). This tendency is grounded in a double critique: first, of the cinematic mechanism as such, which is said to be part of an extensive, ongoing sociocultural project of making certain configurations of visual representation guarantors of knowledge; and, second, of classical narrative, which is said to depend on the security of the look as knowledge. It is thus proposed that classical cinema addresses the spectator by means of promoting a kind of textual empiricism, and that this kind of cinema can be demystified by attacking a dominant ideology of vision.

What a description of classical cinema in terms of a Lukácsian aesthetic can lead to, however, is an argument that a more complex conception of filmic address is necessary. The security of the look in classical cinema is used for certain purposes not always, fully, or necessarily achieved by that security, and it may well be a mistake to separate these purposes from the analysis of the interpellating strategies at work. Even if the knowledge we obtain from a narrative is grounded on a secure look, this need not imply that knowledge itself is visible. Just as for Lukács the historian and the novelist have the problem of demonstrating general truths of history not normally observable, so in classical cinema do our observations often, perhaps always in tendency, lead us toward more general or abstract ideas—even sometimes, probably indicatively, to God. (Recall the end of *Birth of a Nation*, where religious allegory is the culmination of this model classical historical film.)

For Lukács (the) meaning (of history) is not directly observable. Similarly, in classical cinema meaning takes the ultimate form of general truths, principles and forces. To assume that classical cinema presents such meaning within the terms of a simple-minded empiricism of vision is to simplify this matter tremendously. In fact, it can result in a *de facto* bracketing of our investigation of psychic investment in the look from questions of ideological interpellation.

None of this is meant to be a rejection of the critique of the ideology of vision. But if we *look at* (and *listen to*) a film in such a way as to gain secure knowledge, the nature of that knowledge—*its* appeal—cannot simply be split from the investigation of perceptual investment. Of course, an interest in Oedipus and family romance narratives helps to overcome such dangers. However, there is still the question of the interpenetration of these discourses with other discourses. As I have been attempting to demonstrate, one of the chief among these other discourses may well be historiographic. Hence, we come again to the historiographic Imaginary.

5

The broad coincidence sketched above between the appearance of the cinematic apparatus and certain elements of its dominant practices on the one hand, and a major historiographic transition on the other hand, is of evident interest for approaching a historiographic Imaginary. The historical significance of this coincidence may not be immediately decidable, but consideration of it can lead to enlightening comparisons among some of the forms taken by historiographic interpellation, not only as history appears in classical cinema but also in historiography proper. Ideally, a full treatise on this topic would be required at this point, but here a few notes must suffice as a conclusion.

For proper historiographic texts there is a pull towards explanation based on general statements and concepts.[14] The attempt to resist this pull was in fact a component of the crisis of historicism in Germany—precisely a crisis of secure subjective position from which one could identify and appeal to such general truths in order to impute meaning to history. The classical narrative text (naturalized in dominant cinema as well as other practices) also registers a pull towards explanation based on general truths. It offers the audience a safe position from which to observe an *histoire* with certainty in order to learn—or to have confirmed—the truth(s) embodied in it. This is what is highlighted by analyzing a classical cinematic aesthetic for Lukácsian components: the link between narrative and historiography is on the grounds of knowledge—that certainty of one or more general truths, explanation, a secure perspective on history. This is not only to reaffirm the centrality of ideological formations in mainstream cinema; it is also an important indication of the character of ideological contestation in historiography proper.

It is at this point that a traditional difficulty presents itself. It might be argued that to link so closely aspects of socially dominant narrative procedures and historiography as ideological practice is ultimately to call into question the very possibility of a historiography which we would want to treat as knowledge, for such a linkage collapses historiographic procedures into textuality and 'mere' ideology. A response would have to propose that there is no such thing as a discourse without the Imaginary and ideology, but that the full absence of these is not 'the' criterion for 'knowledge.' The problem is thus not one of discovering a means of isolating a discourse from its social ground, but rather of conceptualizing and evaluating competing alternatives.

What theoretical framework can be used as a foundation for conceptualizing struggle in historiographic position and knowledge? Lukács' conception of historical knowledge still has a certain attractiveness, but the Althusserian critique of humanist Marxism retains its force against Lukács as a social theory of the epistemological subject. In addition, the Brechtian critique of the ideological implications of classical narrative procedures, which Lukács valorized as historiographic tools, still seems to apply. The Lukácsian notion of a totalizing perspective on history assured by correct compositional practices thus will not in itself provide a solution. Yet the space of general concepts and statements as operative truths for historiography, and hence a certain positionality, cannot just be left vacant. To begin with, to assert that historiography cannot be extricated from ideological processes is not necessarily to argue against *any* historiography, unless one believes in some kind of purified, asocial ideal of knowledge. In that case, simply abandoning the problem is a move which could only be constituted as an untroubled return to German historicism or to an extreme positivism of atomic particulars. Theoretically unsupportable, it can also be attacked as ideologically undesirable. Conceiving, as it does, of historiographic position as impossible, it would permit no contest on the level of historiographic interpellation.

It might be suggested that the grounds and/or character of historiographic interpellation should therefore not be abandoned, but shifted. Thus, for example, just as many now find it attractive to read Brecht as being fertile for work on subject-positioning, perhaps we should pursue a 'Brechtian' conception of historiography. However, this requires considering the place of general historical truths in Brecht's aesthetic theories, and some care is needed. It is correct to say that Brecht discussed the displacement of the spectator from the 'single track' of Aristotelian theater in order to make reception more complex. But even if we substitute 'Lukácsian cinema' for Aristotelian theater, we must note a fundamental aspect of Brecht's thought: Brecht has a positive moment, a position from which to judge the displacements for which he calls. That secure moment is precisely a concept of historical processes as determined by class struggle. For Brecht there is a direction to history, and any transformation of subjectivity can only be promoted on the basis of a certain position on and in history. This is to say that there is a point of security and explanation in Brecht's theoretical writings. That security is very much like an epistemological security, and it is inseparable from the positing of a future. Brecht's arguments and artistic strategies are in fact founded on and have as their purpose the indication of a certain historical possibility, a certain kind of future.[15]

Now, we need not conceptualize this future as the inevitable *telos* that might be presented in a classical cause-effect narrative chain. Such a teleological perspective is what achieves a sophisticated description as history in Lukács and falls to the Althusserian critique, and it is what achieves a popularized embodiment as story in the classical cinema and is challenged by the Brechtian denaturalization. But neither should we be led to some kind of perpetual displacement of positionality, for this refusal is part of the power of Brecht's anti-traditionalism. The need to posit a future implicitly indicates an ideologically crucial site for Brecht, and it can serve to respond to certain key elements of theoretical texts which have had great impact in film theory over the past decade. Examples range from Althusser's insistence that the critique of the subject should not lead to a simple evacuation of the 'ethico-political' domain controlled by humanist ideologies, to Barthes' beginning *S/Z* from what he calls 'evaluation.'[16]

It is, in fact, the evaluative moment which is one of the great strengths of Marxism as a conception of history. Marxism provides, at least in theory and at least in some of its variants, a provisional positionality based on the possibility of a different kind of future. This is what supplies a means for distinguishing a historiographical Imaginary of something we could take as a knowledge. This is to say, finally, that if one attempts a brief, clear conceptualization of historiography, the result may seem simplistic: the study of stasis *and transformation* of social formations (and this encompasses the study of various sectors of social formations, such as the production of images and sounds). But this formulation does affirm a basic insight of historical materialism, namely the identity of historiographic and political analyses as areas of ideological practice intertwining with claims of knowledge. It is in such claims that the discourse of the dominant cinema intersects with other discourses. This paper has been an exploration of such an intersection in the area of historiography itself.

Metz has told us that the cinema is an imaginary signifier, in part because of the way it presents an absence to our perception. If this is so, there are parallels in historiography. Heath points out that historiography, too, is founded on presenting us with an absence, namely that of the represented past; however, it must be added that there is also the implicit absence of a represented future. It is this absent future as much as the absent past which is the foundation of a historiographic Imaginary of a knowledge.

NOTES

1. I am grateful to David Bordwell, Edward Branigan and Seymour Chatman for comments on earlier versions of this paper.
The terms introduced above have all had wide use in certain sectors of film study over the past several years. They appear in this paper with varying degrees of theoretical rigor, so it may be useful to define them as they will be employed:
Ideology as used here is not intended to connote a sharp break with 'science' or 'knowledge,' but rather the complex intertwining of that which we must take as knowledge with its social ground in the domain of representation.
Interpellation is a term used by both Barthes and Althusser. It roughly designates the pulling of individuals into social positions addressed by discursive entities as institutions. See Roland Barthes, *Mythologies*, trans. Annette Lavers (New York: Hill & Wang, 1972), pp. 124-125; and Louis Althusser, 'Ideology and Ideological State Apparatuses (Notes towards an Investigation),' in *Lenin and Philosophy and Other Essays*, trans. Ben Brewster (New York: Monthly Review Press, 1971), especially pp. 170-183.
The Lacanian concept of *the Imaginary* is used in a broad sense, to indicate the aspects of a discursive entity that strive toward closure, unity and the consequent reassuring of the (masterful) position of the addressee.

2. Important contributions to this project already exist. See, for example, Hayden White, *Metahistory: The Historical Imagination in Nineteenth-Century Europe* (Baltimore, MD: Johns Hopkins University Press, 1973); Hayden White, 'The Value of Narrativity in the Representation of Reality,' *Critical Inquiry*, vol. 7, no. 1 (1980), pp. 5-27; and Fredric Jameson, *The Political Unconscious: Narrative as a Socially Symbolic Act* (Ithaca, NY: Cornell University Press, 1981).

3. Stephen Heath, 'Contexts,' *Edinburgh Magazine*, no. 2 (1977), pp. 37-43. The term *histoire* is, of course, the French word which (rather conveniently) can be translated either as 'story' or as 'history.' It has taken on a certain technical significance both in linguistics and narrative analysis. See Geoffrey Nowell-Smith, 'A Note on History/Discourse,' *Edinburgh Magazine*, no. 1 (1976), pp. 26-32.

4. Georg C. Iggers, *The German Conception of History: The National Tradition of Historical Thought from Herder to the Present* (Middletown, CT: Wesleyan University Press, 1968), pp. 124-125.

5. Richard Hofstadter, *The Progressive Historians: Turner, Beard, Parrington* (New York: Alfred A. Knopf, 1969), p. 35.

6. See, for example, Colin MacCabe, 'Realism and the Cinema: Notes on Some Brechtian Theses,' *Screen*, vol. 15, no. 2 (1974), pp. 7-27; and Stephen Heath, 'Narrative Space,' in

Questions of Cinema (London: Macmillan & Co., 1981), pp. 19-75. Note that this general claim about cinema and narrative has to do with sociocultural functioning, and not an ontological characteristic or 'nature' of cinema which would make it somehow inherently a narrative medium; hence, the kind of complaints Durgnat raises concerning Metz' association of cinema with narrative are here beside the point. Raymond Durgnat, 'Film Theory: From Narrative to Description,' *Quarterly Review of Film Studies*, vol. 7, no. 2 (1982), pp. 109-127.

7. A varying number of elements of this kind of account of Griffith's career, *Birth of a Nation*, and *Intolerance* can be found in several works, including: Lewis Jacobs, *The Rise of the American Film: A Critical History* (New York: Teachers College Press, 1968), pp. 199-201; Arthur Knight, *The Liveliest Art: A Panoramic History of the Movies* (New York: New American Library, 1957), pp. 31-37 (this section, symptomatically entitled 'D.W. Griffith: The Father of Film Technique,' is a source which brings together many of the motifs mentioned above); Kenneth MacGowan, *Behind the Screen: The History and Techniques of the Motion Picture* (New York: Delta Books, 1967), pp. 151-153; Paul O'Dell, *Griffith and the Rise of Hollywood* (New York: A.S. Barnes, 1970), pp. 36-39, 84-92; and Robert Sklar, *Movie-Made America: A Cultural History of the Movies* (New York: Random House, 1975), pp. 60-64. For the beginnings of a different kind of approach, which would take Griffith's status both in the film industry of his time and in film historiography as an economically and socioculturally overdetermined datum of film history, see Tom Gunning, 'Weaving a Narrative: Style and Economic Background in Griffith's Biograph Films,' *Quarterly Review of Film Studies*, vol. 6, no. 1 (1981), pp. 11-25.

8. There is a striking coincidence of phrase in another analysis of a film directed by Raoul Walsh: Thomas Clark, '*White Heat*: The Old and the New,' *Wide Angle*, vol. 1, no. 1 (1976; rev. 1979), pp. 60-65. However, the terminology is employed in a different way.

9. Jameson, *The Political Unconscious*, p. 97. Jameson argues for a dialectical double reading which would take into account not only the regressive aspects of nationhood, but also the anticipatory, utopian appeal of nationalism. He treats representations of the nation as (among other things) allegorical figures for a genuinely harmonious collectivity of the future. While there are serious difficulties with his formulation, it has clear relevance for my conclusion below. See also pp. 289-299.

10. See MacCabe, 'Realism and the Cinema.'

11. Georg Lukács, *The Historical Novel*, trans. Hannah and Stanley Mitchell (Boston, MA: Beacon Press, 1963), pp. 17-89.

12. Bertolt Brecht, 'Against Georg Lukács,' in Ernst Bloch *et al.*, *Aesthetics and Politics* (London: New Left Books, 1977), pp. 68-85.

13. Stephen Heath, 'Lessons from Brecht,' *Screen*, vol. 15, no. 2 (1974), pp. 103-128. See especially, for example, p. 113.

14. It is of relevance to note that in many accounts of historical explanation, this pull towards the general is taken as logically valid. For example, within analytical philosophy a dominant object of debate has been the importance of the general 'covering law' of a syllogistic structure of explanation, made famous by Hempel. Compare Walsh's notion of a 'colligatory concept,' which is another kind of generality (a concept as opposed to a proposition) formulated against Hempel with explicit reference to Hegel. See Carl G. Hempel, 'The Function of General Laws in History,' reprinted in *Theories of History*, ed. Patrick Gardiner (Glencoe, IL: The Free Press, 1959), pp. 344-356; and W.H. Walsh, 'Colligatory Concepts in History,' in *The Philosophy of History*, ed. Patrick Gardiner (New York: Oxford University Press, 1974), pp. 127-144. The latter is a revision of an article that originally appeared in *Studies in the Nature and Teaching of History*, ed. W.H. Burston and D. Thompson (London: Routledge & Kegan Paul, 1967), pp. 65-84. This notion of a pull towards the general is of great importance for the topics here under discussion, but full elaboration of its implications is beyond the scope of this paper.

15. For example, in 'A Short Organum for the Theatre,' Brecht writes: '[Dialectical materialism] regards nothing as existing except insofar as it changes, in other words is in disharmony with itself. . . . [Man (sic)] does not have to stay the way he is now, nor does he have to be seen only as he is now, but also as he might become. We must not start with him, we must start on him. This means, however, that I must not simply set myself in his place, but set myself facing him, to represent us all. That is why the theatre must alienate what it shows.' *Brecht on Theatre: The Development of an Aesthetic*, trans. and ed. John Willett (New York: Hill & Wang, 1964), p. 193.

16. Louis Althusser, *For Marx*, trans. Ben Brewster (New York: Vintage Books, 1970), pp. 230-231; Roland Barthes, *S/Z*, trans. Richard Miller (New York: Hill & Wang, 1974), pp. 3-4. I have argued elsewhere for the utility of Barthes' notion of writing (*écriture*) for a historical approach to signification: Philip Rosen, 'The Politics of the Sign and Film Theory,' *October*, no. 17 (1981), especially pp. 13-17.

Italian Film and American Capital, 1947-1951

Michael Silverman

It is difficult to know where Italian 'neo-realist' film and the literature accompanying it goes wrong. In a formalist film history each film would take its place in a diachronic unfolding which is always in a state of becoming until that moment when the end point is reached, though there could be occasional interpolations which suggest the modification of an essence ('neo-realism,' perhaps) never explained but invoked as transcendental standard. Such a history might point to the incursion of the miraculous: De Sica-Zavattini's *Miracle in Milan* (1950) would then be a film which indicates a despair attaching to concrete solutions, a yearning for metaphysical intervention; or Rossellini's *La Macchina Ammazzacattivi* (1948) would stand as a critique of using the apparatuses of representation (specifically the camera) as a means of social redress. Both films would be seen as violating the 'spirit of neo-realism' as an aspiration for cinema's direct involvement with political processes and social change, instances culminating in a 'break' from this 'spirit' at some later point, a point at which everyone (all formalist historians) might agree (*La Strada* [1954], perhaps, or *Nights of Cabiria* [1956]), and for which many instances might be furnished.[1]

In those film histories whose primary emphasis is on the political allegiances which support the texts and which are reflected or refracted by them, the stress would be on the unfolding of an ideological formation seen as a 'partial and historic' set of social and textual positions. In the case of Italian film production from 1945 through 1954—*Rome, Open City* to *Senso*—a diachronic unfolding would document an increasing erasure of contradiction from the texts themselves, a slackening of any dialectical relation between the images on the screen and the social space inhabited by the spectators, and the weakening of the political left accompanied by the solidification of the petty bourgeoisie and monopoly capital.[2] Such a history is easy to write in postwar Europe, and in Italian film culture it traces itself up through a few textual dead ends, for example De Sica-Zavattini's *Il Tetto* (1956), before a film such as *Accattone* (1961) 'arrives' to effect a specific critique of the enterprise of neo-realism as a whole.[3]

For an American viewer coming to these films through recent theory there are, of course, further problems. Since the voluminous writings in Italian which contain much of the ideological struggle remain untranslated, the essays of André Bazin in the fourth volume of *Qu'est-ce que le cinéma?* are still, after twenty years, the central theoretical articulation on Italian neo-realism for most viewers and the major point of entry into the films. To the extent that Bazin's 'aesthetic of reality' has been seen as an idealist expression supporting dominant notions of social representation, it has come to stand for what Colin MacCabe and others have shown to be an 'inability to investigate contradiction.'[4] As Bazin has been seen more and more as a conservative idealist, spokesperson for an aesthetic quietism, the very texts upon which he lavished so much attention have themselves become suspect, making an important period in a nation's film practice a burned-out ground. If the production processes of these films as presented to the viewer seem unproblematic, free from those crises of subjectivity which mark Hollywood melodrama (to refer to a currently favored mode), it may have to do with the way most of these films systematically disavow reference to the production of social realism and political formation, naturalize their own terms of production as well as—exactly as—the production of the social field within which they reside historically.

Two contrary examples: it is in fact as easy to mount an ideological critique of the alliance between the Church and left-wing anti-fascism as depicted in *Rome, Open City* as it is to critique, say, the relationship between the father and his family in Sirk's *There's Always Tomorrow*. In both cases the text constructs an ambiguous wish, a tenuous harmony which the viewer is forced to read as both unnatural and necessary, if not particularly fortuitous. Alliances are seen as circumstantial, above all as a matter of social construction. The viewer may well wish to route the text back toward that construction, to investigate the manner in which both text and viewer have been constructed. But in the works especially prized by Bazin—the Po delta segment of *Paisan* (1946) or *Bicycle Thieves* (1945), for example—all avenues for the discovery of contradiction have been sealed by the text. That is the text's labor, presented as the operation of the natural . The very material quality of the shot in *Rome, Open City* manifestly changes during the interrogation sequence, molding the partisan as a religious martyr through the use of close-ups and low-key lighting, the scene marked off as a

'Hollywood fantasy.'[5] In the final segment of *Paisan*, however, as Bazin carefully demonstrates, 'considered in itself, each image being nothing more than a fragment of reality preceding all meaning, the whole surface of the screen should manifest an equally concrete "density." '[6] It is very difficult to effect a material critique with such a density of repression offering the spectator 'a certain mode of entry into what is presented on the screen' with the image thus presented being 'in some sense beyond argument.'[7]

In addition to the legacy of Bazin's privileging of these films (certain of them, at any rate),[8] we must face a widely-held skepticism about the nature of historical writing, even indeed that writing which seems to pit itself discursively over against 'historical writing,' but which cannot escape its shadow. The notorious conclusion to Hindess and Hirst's *Pre-Capitalist Modes of Production* sounds the warning note:

> The concepts of the modes of production developed here do not form a history in thought, mirroring in their succession the evolution of the real. The field of application of these concepts is not history. We reject the notion of history as a coherent and worthwhile object of study. These concepts are abstract, their value is not limited by the analysis of the concrete. As concepts they can have a theoretical function even if concrete conditions to which they are pertinent do not exist, have not existed and will not exist.[9]

Any attempt to confront theory with the real (or with a specific social formation) as a means of assessing theory will be labelled 'empiricism.' In failing to dissociate history from any 'real object' whatsoever, Althusser, for example, is said to have provided us with a shadow writing of history, however great his struggles against Hegelian purposiveness. Balibar's introduction of 'transitional' production into his theories of structural causality is then a sentimental and 'absurd' genuflection to some notion of the 'real,' in which transitions 'do occur': his writing thus amounts to 'a rationalisation and reconstruction of what it takes to be a real object.'[10]

The warnings against writing which may purport to be the presentation of a social formation in process but which in fact tends to reintroduce an essentialist category at a more removed, more abstract level, are well taken. At the same time, they make us nervous about any explanation which may introduce historical intervention in any guise, even at the level of event. In an attempt to modify Hindess and Hirst's strictures, Geoffrey Nowell-Smith puts in a guarded and slightly ironical disclaimer:

> I would maintain . . . that a practice of historical enquiry is not reducible to a dependence on [causal] models and is in no way invalidated by the emergence of the new and not-so-new structuralising procedures, and that historians can—and to some extent have [sic]—develop a practice

of tracing connections between phenomena which both takes account of the new principles and yet retains a specificity as history, that is to say (minimally) a concern with problems which arise out of the fact of there having been a past.[11]

But before outlining Nowell-Smith's proposed 'practice of tracing connections between phenomena,' two recent modes of historical procedure need at least to be mentioned.

The first—what has become known as studies of 'popular memory'— initiates a movement away from an idealized teleology and attempts to insert into discursive production a series of fallible utterances and impressions, which would formerly have been consigned to a ghetto of 'raw material,' from which history would then have been constructed. Apart from the tendency here to valorize the literary and expressive elements of the texts found or produced,[12] inevitably reaffirmed is a reified set of class relations whereby the working class, and/or individuals speaking from within it, tend to 'produce' their lives as memory for readers who are usually intellectuals.[13] This procedure has involved a tendency to diminish awareness of the mechanisms productive of memory, controlling and monitoring it, which suggests that in order for this area of historical expression to have real validity, the apparatuses themselves will have to be named and analyzed more fully.[14]

In addition to the claims of proponents of 'popular memory'—that as a category it restores a 'lost' or 'repressed' history in such a way as to counter the self-guaranteeing claims of dominant historical writing[15]—it emphasizes its difference from the merely decorative, retrospective/ retrogressive methods of presenting history as a series of luxurious 'views,' prospects which suggest the perpetual availability of the past through the emulation of a certain style.[16] Yet the number of unexamined mediating procedures—relations of subject to event, the role of the recording apparatus, the place of the viewing subject—forces almost immediately the reconstitution of familiar assumptions and practices. Foucault's statement that 'popular memory' constitutes one more theft by the bourgeoisie from the working class of their history may seem too partisan; at the same time, it is hard to avoid thinking that a concept like 'popular memory' seeks to reintroduce the 'natural' into a very wearisome and tangled debate, seeming to bypass the troubled status of the 'real' in discursive practice, but restoring it in folkloric ways.

The second mode of historical procedure to which some reference must be made is the recent instance of Fredric Jameson's 'ideology of form.'[17] Building on Poulantzas' distinction between 'mode of production' as a wholly synchronous theoretical entity and a 'social formation' which would entail the description of a given society at a given moment of its development,[18] Jameson skirts the obvious danger of an unbridgeable dichotomy between 'abstract theory' and 'concrete fact' by demanding a set of readings which would pluralize both the readings themselves and the systems under discussion. Jameson suggests that this plurality may already 'exist' somewhere in the social field, and that much writing (and other practice) has tended to unitize this plurality. Even if one were to say that the plurality does not 'exist,' the job of historical writing would be the diacritical introduction of contradiction which might produce such a plurality. Blending Poulantzas and Bloch, Jameson's reference to a 'cultural revolution' which would destabilize habit and writing, value systems and conceptual apparatuses, applies not only to transitional periods like China in the mid-1960s (which may in fact lead to increased social conservatism) but also to a disruption and deferral of coding procedures, beyond distinctions of synchrony and diachrony, toward a history grounded in a determinate practice seeking precisely to resist thematization or reification:

> We may suggest such a possibility obliquely by attention to what the Aristotelians would call the generic satisfaction specific to the form of the great movements of historiography, or what the semioticians might call the 'history-effect' of such narrative texts. Whatever the raw material on which historiographic form works (and we will here only touch on that most widespread type of material which is the sheer chronology of fact as it is produced by the rote-drill of the history manual), the 'emotion' of great historiographic form can then always be seen as the radical restructuration of that inert material, in this instance the powerful reorganization of otherwise inert chronological and 'linear' data in the form of Necessity: why what happened (at first received as 'empirical' fact) had to happen the way it did. From this perspective, then, causality is only one of the possible tropes by which this formal restructuration can be achieved, although it has obviously been a privileged and historically significant one.[19]

Jameson's formulation would see the cinema institution as a 'possible trope' within a large and shifting social field. Within this trope, highly specifiable sub-tropes, what Nowell-Smith calls 'lineages,' might be adumbrated.[20] Each constituency within this trope 'cinema' would invoke 'a study of its own history as a never totally autonomous component of a shifting pattern of combinations.'[21] No history of cinema could be written, except as an infinite yet determinate interweaving of tropes exerting formative pressure on each other in particular and specifiable ways.

In order for what follows—a few tropes about Italian cinema in 1947 and 1948—to be properly organized, it would be necessary to present in some detail a set of historical circumstances, instances within discourse, in order to take them up again in their several pertinent relations to other parts of the social field then and now, to other elements of Italian and American film production, to the implementation of American capital, and (in this case) to the employment of sexuality as a means of diverting attention from other elements of social production. A rigorously detailed example of this kind of analysis is clearly beyond the scope of this paper, but a sketch along these lines may be useful here.

From 1945 through 1947 the Italian film industry could barely survive financially. It is estimated that during this period—from *Rome, Open City* to *La Terra Trema* (1948)—less than ten million lire of 'native' capital were invested in Italian films. What was produced had no overseas market, although *Rome, Open City* had occasional 'prestige' screenings abroad. During these years De Gasperi and the Christian Democratic Party were engaged in a bitter struggle for the consolidation of economic and political power. The corporate structures of Finsider and the IRI—Istituto per la Ricostruzione Industriale—(under which the RAI—Radio Audizione Italiane—for example, was grouped) were left largely intact. Indeed, many of the corporate heads who had tacitly condoned or enthusiastically supported Mussolini retained their power under the tripartite government presided over by De Gasperi. The structure of the cinema industry must be folded into that of a monopolistic economy desperately short of capital, with high unemployment in all industries (chemical, automobile, rubber) ostensibly free from state control but largely dependent upon direct and oblique subsidies.[22] But while other industries remained localized (Fiat, for example, never had to 'relocate' from its base in Turin), in 1942-43 the fascists had literally taken the cinema economy northward to Salo. With the production center south of Rome and the bureaucratic apparatus in Rome itself abandoned, production amazingly continued in the north up to the last days of the regime. The arrival of American troops found Cinecittà intact but deserted.

Many statements by Rossellini, Zavattini and others have demonstrated their reluctance to utilize the facilities of production so fully associated with fascism.[23] Yet it is clear that this was less a matter of authorial choice (whether at the aesthetic or political level—and the two are clearly divorced, at least in Rossellini) than a deliberate blockage of production money by the dominant group within the ruling government hegemony until such time as any money could be safely invested in an ideologically 'stable' product. Here, of course, divisions on the left were particularly helpful; for example, the PCI's (the Italian Communist Party) withdrawal of financial support from Visconti's planned trilogy of films which were to depict the emergence of Southern working-class consciousness within its various conditions of exploitation had much to do with Togliatti's distrust of Gramscian tendencies within the Party. At the same time, Togliatti was playing an ultimately futile game of accommodation with De Gasperi, systematically scorning Parri's

Action Party and isolating Nenni's Socialists by making them seem, incredibly, more likely to cause social unrest than the communists. The original script of Visconti's trilogy did indeed have a 'strongly revolutionary content' and this alone would have been sufficient for the Party to make sure that the funding would come finally from Universalia with its close ties to the Christian Democrats and the Vatican.[24]

Thus each Italian film from this volatile period must be read through the struggle for political power on the left and in the center, and through an economic situation which channelled capital away from certain key sectors of the social field not because these sectors were undervalued (cinema, as opposed to chemicals), but precisely because their importance was seen as crucial to the articulation of social procedures and because strong contestation was occurring within them. De Gasperi himself perceived the importance of cinema, its potential for ensuring discursive hegemony:

> As a medium it is unparalleled for its reflection and definition of Italian
> life. Our party must encourage its growth, nourish its artists and seek to
> instill the very highest standards in those who produce it.[25]

But the policy seems to have been (1) to avoid any active participation in production which might have mobilized the left into a counter-cinema; (2) to keep money diverted into other areas of social production; (3) to wait for those few investment companies willing to risk venture capital on film to dry up; and then (4) to control the American money which was seen as inevitably arriving and in expectation of which the shrewd Einaudi implemented his selective policies of deflation.[26]

American money intervened significantly in Italy starting in 1948, the first year of funding under the Marshall Plan. It was a four-year plan, technically called the European Recovery Program (ERP). Strikes by the left, designed to call attention to impending American influence, were crushed in the fall of 1947. The results of the general election of April, 1948 were never in doubt, since the question posed was one of 'recovery' with capital or 'isolation' without it.[27] Almost immediately the influx of this new money began to be felt within Italian film production. It would be instructive (necessary, one would think) to analyze the relations between capital and representation for each film produced during the first four years of ERP funding. The brief scope of this paper permits the sketching-in of only one example.[28]

Riso amaro (*Bitter Rice*, 1948) was an attempt to focus on the working conditions of itinerant female agricultural laborers in the Po valley. The original script was written by three members of the PCI with backgrounds as critics—Giuseppe De Santis, Carlo Lizzani and Gianni Puccini. In the script the women form a kind of lumpen proletariat waiting for some form of social organization. De Santis recalls that he spent the spring of 1947 working with the women and talking to them:

> 'After all, at that time there was terrible unemployment in all areas of the economy, but especially for women, many of whom had lost their men during the war—whether the men were soldiers or partisans it doesn't matter—and who under fascism had been thoroughly repressed and domesticated, so that they had no skills, only their bodies, which they were of course forced to sell, in one way or another.'[29]

During De Santis' stay, the large agricultural co-ops initially formed under fascism attempted further to exploit the women by bringing in hundreds of day-laborers willing to work without the usual 'seasonal' contract of forty days' labor for forty kilos of rice and a salary of forty thousand lire. The PCI sent union organizers to help the contracted laborers, and the co-ops called in the police:

> 'Well, looking back on it I can see that it was a familiar enough scenario. But we wanted to show that the Party hadn't really thought through its position on all this, too. I mean, why were they so willing to support these miserable conditions? I suppose, though, that some class consciousness might have emerged. And we tried to show this in the script, tried to show them coming to some position a little to the left— you might say—of the Party, of its organizers, at any rate.'

With the script completed, De Santis attempted to raise production money from the Party:

> 'They were nervous, nervous about everything. They weren't sure how Visconti's work would turn out, they weren't sure if they should be involved with cinema at all. The story was talked about, they said it was "important," but they finally turned it down. They sat in their office. I think finally they were more concerned about what De Gasperi might think.'

After making the rounds of various independent producers, De Santis received a telephone call from Dino De Laurentiis:

> 'He called me, I didn't call him. I was aware of him, of course, Ponti too, they were just getting started. He told me he had heard about the project and was interested. We arranged a meeting. When I got to his office, there were three writers with him. He said that the only way the film could be made was to ensure a global release, by which he meant the U.S. And he said that the Banco di Roma would arrange an American investment in the project through Lux.'

De Santis argued that the project had meaning only within the terms of a specific struggle, that to make it an 'international' film would be to rob it of any social context. Ultimately he was faced with the inevitable choice—accept American money and influence or not make the film at all. Lacking institutional support from the left, De Santis and the others initially involved in the project accepted the compromise. Even a mildly symptomatic reading of the film today easily reveals the moments of investment and diversion, the capital outlay revolving around and anchored in the body of Silvana Mangano, the terms of the melodrama covering and smoothing the text at every moment when a specific issue threatens to demand further investigation.

American money funnelled through the Banco di Roma, overseen by the Christian Democrats through the ERP; the opening of Cinecittà; the regularization of production; the return to the star system; costume films; the international style of the early 1960s—reading the image in the light of organization of capital, the processing of local political issues onto the grid of international production, should be done with every film. Not film history, then, but film read within a series of intersecting discourses, each of which may have its own irregular unfolding. The film becomes a matrix within which these unfoldings may momentarily be held and studied, even at the level of shot-by-shot analysis. Mangano in *Riso amaro* walks left of frame through a rice paddy perpendicular to an undifferentiated mass of less strikingly attractive women, all of whom are bent over their work. As she moves to the middle distance she raises her skirt out of the water to just below her buttocks. Our eyes no longer watch the right side of the frame, the mass of working women, but take in the movement of the skirt, the revelation once again of the body. Not only voyeurism and the gaze, not only the Bazinian middle distance, but the documentable trace of American capital investment is marked by the movement of that skirt.

NOTES

1. Histories of this sort vary greatly in quality. Many have useful information and evocative summaries. See, alphabetically: Roy Armes, *Patterns of Realism* (South Brunswick, NJ: A.S. Barnes, 1971); Fabio Carpi, *Cinema italiano del dopoguerra* (Milan: Schwartz, 1958); Pierre Leprohon, *Le Cinéma italien* (Paris: Editions Seghers, 1966); Vinicio Marinucci, *Tendenze del cinema italiano* (Rome: Unitalia Film, 1959); Brunello Rondi, *Il neorealismo italiano* (Parma: Guanda, 1956). The most contested and important work remains that of Guido Aristarco; see *Miti e relalà nel cinema italiano* (Milan: Il Soggiatore, 1961).

2. See Mario Cannella, 'Ideology and Aesthetic Hypotheses in the Criticism of Neo-Realism,' *Screen*, vol. 14, no. 4 (1973-1974), pp. 5–60, for a history of the revisional work of such writers as Amendola, Fortini, Basso and others, and its relation to the 'writing' of neo-realist theory.

3. Many critics (Fink, Chiarini, and others) note the posing of Accattone against a background of slum high-rises as a shot which directly contradicts the final shot of *Rome, Open City*, in which children descending to the city are posed against the background of buildings dominated by St. Peter's.

4. Colin MacCabe, 'Principles of Realism and Pleasure,' *Screen*, vol. 15, no. 2 (1974), p. 19.

5. Robert Burgoyne, 'The Imaginary and the Neo-Real,' *Enclitic*, vol. 3, no. 1 (1979), p. 18. This study characterizes the torture sequence as an hallucination 'in which neo-realism is modulated and distorted to allow the production of symbolic and imaginary patterning of space, meaning, vision.' (p. 19.) 'Neo-realism' is here employed, not without a certain self-consciousness, as a term of transcendental meaning, from which the torture sequence is then seen as varying significantly. Burgoyne points to 'the existence and functioning of some sort of censorship analogous to that which constrains the dreamwork [in Freud].' (p. 17.) That repression seen as censorship in psychoanalytic terms may simultaneously be a pressure felt in the text at those moments (such as this one) when the partisan and the priest are being organized into a fellowship of action which precisely prevents any clarification of the political contradictions inherent in such an alliance.

6. André Bazin, *Qu'est-ce que le cinéma?*, vol. IV (Paris: Editions du Cerf, 1962), p. 34.

7. MacCabe, 'Within a Rossellini film . . . if we are continually aware of our presence in the cinema (particularly in his historical films)—that presence itself is not questioned in any way.' (p. 20.)

8. One must note, of course, the presence of another idealist discourse, that of authorship. The films discussed in *Qu'est-ce que le cinéma?*, vol. IV, are primarily those of Rossellini, De Sica and Fellini, secondarily those of Visconti and Castellani. No extensive discussion is given over to more socially committed directors like Vergano, De Santis, Lattuada (at that time) and others.

9. Barry Hindess and Paul Q. Hirst, *Pre-Capitalist Modes of Production* (London: Routledge & Kegan Paul, 1975), p. 321.

10. Hindess and Hirst, p. 320.

11. Geoffrey Nowell-Smith, 'On the Writing of the History of the Cinema: Some Problems,' *Edinburgh Magazine*, no. 2 (1977), p. 10.

12. See Claire Johnston's critique in *Edinburgh Magazine*, no. 2 (1977) pp. 18-19. Memorial re-creation has of course been a crucial element of much textual production (the 'case history') and of a certain form of sociological 'finding,' ranging from poeticized renderings (such as the Agee-Evans evocation of rural Southern life during the Great Depression, *Let Us Now Praise Famous Men* [Boston, MA: Houghton Mifflin Co., 1980]), to purported 'documentation' (as in the 'narratives' of Oscar Lewis, for example *The Children of Sanchez* [New York: Random House, 1966]).

13. For a typical case of intellectual bad conscience and hyperbole evoked by this trap, see Pasolini's comments on the narrativizing of several peasant lives as 'an essential contribution to postwar literature,' in *Le belle bandiere* (Rome: Editori riuniti, 1977), p. 202.

14. Michel Foucault has noted that 'a whole number of apparatuses have been set up . . . to obstruct the flow of this popular memory. And it could be said that this attempt has been pretty successful.' (*Cahiers du cinéma*, no. 252 [1974], p. 22.)

15. 'Distinct from the contemporary concern with the past, a concern which is associated with a nostalgic recovery of a past through a recreation of its paraphernalia, the notion of Popular Memory seeks to fix those films which use history in the construction of their narrative, drawing on the facticity of the past to assure the veracity of their statements.' (Keith Tribe, 'History and the Production of Memories,' *Screen*, vol. 18, no. 4, [1977-1978], p. 13.)

16. The initial critique of Malle's *Lacombe, Lucien* (1974) and Cavani's *Il portiere di notte* (1973) as 'retro' texts in *Cahiers du cinéma*, nos. 251-252 (1974) began the re-thinking of the function of 'popular memory.'

17. Fredric Jameson, *The Political Unconscious* (Ithaca, NY: Cornell University Press, 1981), pp. 98ff.

18. Nicos Poulantzas, *Political Power and Social Classes*, (London: New Left Books, 1973), pp. 13-16.

19. Jameson, p. 101.

20. Nowell-Smith, p. 11. Among those cited are: sciences of optics, technical development, capital accumulation, representation, psychoanalysis and specularity, etc.

21. Ibid.

22. For a statistical tabulation of government subsidy in various Italian industries, see *A Century of Economic and Social Development in Italy, 1861-1961* (Rome: Istituto Centrale di Statistica, 1961), especially pp. 127-139. See also Shepard B. Clough, *The Economic History of Modern Italy* (New York: Columbia University Press, 1964) for a wealth of undigested statistical information, especially on Confindustria.

23. See the statements by both in *Il cinema e l'uomo moderno*, ed. Umberto Barbaro (Milan: Edizioni Sociali, 1950), pp. 96-97, 111; Claudio Bertieri, *30 anni di cinema italiano* (Genoa: Circolo Aziendale Cornigliano, 1960), pp. 35ff; and the interviews in *Bianco e nero*, February, 1952 (Rossellini) and June, 1963 (Zavattini).

24. Armes, *Patterns of Realism*, p. 110.

25. Quoted in Mario Einaudi and François Goguel, *Christian Democracy in Italy and France* (Notre Dame, IN: University of Notre Dame Press, 1952), p. 171.

26. The role of Luigi Einaudi (De Gasperi's first Minister of the Budget) in preparing the way for American commercial investment in certain key sectors of the Italian economy needs further study, especially in relation to the field of 'communications,' including subsidies within the film industry. Preliminary work in English has been done by William Diebold, Jr., *Trade and Payments in Western Europe, 1947-1951* (New York: Harper & Brothers, 1952), and *The Schumann Plan: A Study in Economic Cooperation, 1950-1959* (New York: Praeger, 1959).

27. H. Stuart Hughes, *The United States and Italy* (1953; rev. ed. Cambridge, MA: Harvard 1965), p. 147.

28. The major producing unit during the years under scrutiny (1948-1951) was Lux Film: *In nome della legge* (Germi, 1948); *Il mulino del Po* (Lattuada, 1948); *Riso amaro* (De Santis, 1948); *Senza pietà* (Lattuada, 1948); *Non c'e pace tra gli ulivi* (De Santis, 1949); *Il camino della speranza* (Germi, 1950). Lux Film was the main recipient of government subsidy and was set up as a flourishing company after the infusion of ERP funding. Prior to 1948 it had co-produced *Il bandito* (Lattuada, 1946) with De Laurentiis, whose first production this was; *Vivere in pace* (Zampa, 1946), with Ponti's private 'company'; and *L'onorevole Angelina* (Zampa, 1947), with Ora productions.

29. All quotations of De Santis are from private conversations taped in 1973.

Film History and Visual Pleasure: Weimar Cinema

Thomas Elsaesser

> *History has . . . abandoned its attempts to understand events in terms of cause and effect in the formless unity of some great evolutionary process. . . . It did not do this in order to seek out structures anterior to, alien or hostile to the event. It was rather in order to establish those diverse converging, and sometimes divergent, but never autonomous series that enables us to circumscribe the 'locus' of an event, the limits to its fluidity and the conditions of its emergence.*
>
> —Michel Foucault[1]

'Film'/'History'

Every American film studies program teaches courses on film history. One might even say that in the 70s, this was one of *the* 'growth areas' for film scholars. As Robert C. Allen put it:

> We are entering, I think, a period of long called-for film historical introspection . . . and retrospection . . . , the result of which, hopefully, will be nothing short of a complete reassessment of the discipline of film history: a thorough and continuing reexamination of its nature, scope, goals, materials, and methodologies.[2]

In many ways, his confidence and optimism were justified, for remarkable work has been produced, composed of detailed studies as well as ambitious overviews, embodying conceptual reorientation and a high degree of self-reflexivity. So much is being published that it has become difficult, if not impossible, to absorb it all, especially since what is on offer in the film journals, bookshop displays and publishers' catalogues under the now fashionable heading of film history does not merely shade in blank areas in an otherwise agreed-on topography of a common terrain. On the contrary, the best part of the energy in recent writing comes from an awareness of a double front: the polemical dissatisfaction with all those film histories where a consensus is presupposed about what 'film' and 'history' have to do with each other; and a debate among the new generation of film historians about the 'determinants' (demographic, economic, technological, ideological) that might be said to have 'produced' the quantitative changes and permutations of forms on whose account films may lay claim to have a history at all. As Will Straw has pointed out, the pressures to formulate such a history undoubtedly are themselves historical and institutional:

> One recurrent feature of film studies literature . . . has been the expression of malaise over the underdeveloped state of film historiography. . . . This felt necessity for an increased rigor in the writing of film history, however, may be linked in part to the manner in which Film Studies has emerged institutionally as an academic discipline. . . . [It] has served to foreground the absence of a methodological-theoretical foundation for the writing of film history.[3]

As elsewhere in the humanities, the very definition of the 'discipline' is at stake. Why are we seeking to redraw the boundaries of a field that, as is becoming increasingly evident, has taken its contours in the way it did partly because it cannot finally be demarcated from other adjoining academic subjects? An expansion of what is considered pertinent research has gone hand in hand with a call for 'increased rigor': is there not a potential contradiction? Edward Buscombe, paraphrasing Thomas Kuhn, expects 'true scientific advance . . . only upon the formulation of a "paradigm," ' and notes that until then 'we have film historians, but something less than film history.'[4] Yet Charles F. Altman, working 'towards a historiography of the American Film,' comes to the conclusion that:

> [f]ilm history has now reached its second stage: from the who, what, where, and when we have moved to the how and why; from establishing facts we have progressed to explaining facts. Along with this change American film history has broken down into separate schools, each having its own object and methodology, each depending on a different hypothesis about the fundamental determinants of cinema production and distribution, each proposing its own valorizations, its own canon, its own periodization.[5]

Nonetheless, the phrase one occasionally hears about a common 'historiographical project' may not be quite as solemnly mystifying as it sounds. Some kind of coherent shape is becoming visible, though it is one to which the metaphor of the field is perhaps wholly inadequate. Instead, it is more like a sort of stereometric shape in the increasingly conceptual space that history has become, now that we are beginning to learn to live with history's last teleology, 'the end of the world.' But in order to get this astral body into proper view, film history has decisively moved away from films, in particular from film criticism, and toward what used to be called the sociology of film. If film criticism has traditionally limited its object of study to the individual film or a director's work, the sociology of film saw its task in defining genres, movements, periods or, occasionally, the sociocultural significance of a particular national cinema. In contrast to both, the new film history—currently firmly devoted to the 'materialist determinants'—has entrenched itself in economic histories of particular studios and financial cartels, of court actions and patent wars, real-estate deals, popcorn franchises, 'zoning' agreements and fire regulations.

Such empirical research no doubt helps to give the discipline a firm footing. And it is certainly instructive to know that films stand on feet of clay. But does not the excitement over the discovery of so many diverse and hitherto disregarded factors which exerted a shaping influence give rise also to an equivalent disappointment, namely that such a history necessarily accepts the film industry's own (admittedly unacknowledged) relation to its products—as inert commodities, as accumulations of dead labor moving through time and space in order to realize surplus value for an industry that distinguishes itself from other parts of a capitalist economy mainly by the complexity (pleasing to the investigating intelligence) of the social values that enter into the successful product? Could it be that the film industry is not primarily product-oriented, but a service industry? A conceptual shift is certainly in evidence:

> Focusing here on the film industry during the 1930s, one finds that analysts of film/production/ideology accept and utilize [the] concept of finance capitalism. Typically we find in the now famous collective text by the Editors of *Cahiers du cinéma* concerning *Young Mr. Lincoln*: 'As early as 1935 the five major companies . . . and the three minor . . . were totally controlled by bankers and financiers.' This is a crucial assertion because with it the Editors are able to situate Hollywood as an industry within the 1930s U.S. economy and thus provide an explanation of any Hollywood film's place in the capitalist mode of production. . . . I shall argue that finance capitalism does not provide an appropriate conceptual framework for the analysis of film/production/ideology. . . . We should shift our analysis away from the so-called Morgan/Rockefeller financial interest groups to the behavior of giant U.S. corporations, principally intercorporate conflict. A new type of competition exists. These giant monopolists rarely attempt to eliminate each other. All have a major stake in the status quo. Instead the monopolists

struggle to gain the largest share of their industry's surplus (excess) profits.[6]

Film historians like Douglas Gomery—quoted here—do not find their partner in dialogue in the writers of textbook histories, which, like so many generations struck from a poor print of a film classic, have served to pass on and pass off a mere impressionistic succession of moments for the real thing. Instead Gomery is looking towards film theorists ('film/production/ ideology') as his natural allies. They, too, have set themselves firmly against film criticism, preferring to see the individual product as a text, as exemplifying (with some regularity and systematicity) the 'ideological practice,' the 'institutional mode of representation,' the 'apparatus,' 'classical Hollywood narrative,' the 'imaginary signifier'—all recent coinages to point to a differently constituted entity, which is not films, but 'the cinema.'

What the meeting of film theory and film history in the last decade has brought to light is not, in the first instance, how deeply films and the film industry are implicated in and determined by capitalist production or bourgeois ideology. The findings of film history have recently been judged by what they contribute to the history, or histories, of what becomes visible in and through *both* the films *and* the industries that produce the renewable and repeatable side of the cinema experience (i.e., the network of remembered and anticipated, expected or actively pursued sensations and sights). These point not towards a finite object, but, if anywhere, towards a finite subject, namely the spectator, whose desire is what sets in motion all the other machines of the institution cinema. According to John Ellis:

> [f]ilms, then, are themselves processes rather than products: capital is turned over by the industry through people paying to see a film, not to buy a copy of it (i.e., paying for the *possibility* of pleasure). These processes that are films turn upon the perpetual production of representations that are addressed to a viewing subject; they effect a perpetual placing of the subject in relation to desire—a continual process that we are pleased to call pleasurable.[7]

Or as Geoffrey Nowell-Smith puts it: 'film images are part of the stock of images that we pay money to have haunt our minds.'[8]

A History of Pleasure?

Cinema: the institution of a particular kind of pleasure. If the determinants of the cinema are to be sought in the pleasure it organizes in the spectator, in its ability to bind an audience, then the films themselves cannot be the objects of desire. Rare are the cases where a spectator goes to see *The Sound of Music* for the seventy-fifth time, or proudly looks back at having watched *Casablanca* 'at least once a year since it opened.'[9] Cinematic pleasure is 'normally' a very mobile form of cathexis, eminently transferable from object to object under the rule of substitution and repetition, and thus fetishistic. The objects change, the obsession remains the same. Or does it? Certainly, the recognition of such a process of transfer has led to powerful arguments for not confining film history to a history of films. On the other hand, if the pleasure remains the same, what need is there for a history? What in the cinema *is* historical, in the sense of being subject to change, capable of being altered or affected by events, liable to mutations and shifts? Is pleasure historical, or 'only' the spectators and the sites of production that bind them to consumption?

Ellis and Nowell-Smith both voice a certain disquiet about pleasure: what the spectator buys is the '*possibility* of pleasure,' 'images that haunt our minds,' effects which we are 'pleased to call pleasurable.' It all points to the idea that pleasure is itself a composite, something that only makes sense in relation to other terms and thus not an ultimate determinant, a first cause. Pleasure, as it is bound up with signification, representation, meaning, perception and memory, is therefore perforce implicated in history as the shifting and fixing of the relationships between desire and representation, which can be specified even if the question of how these relationships are articulated in the cinema via aural and visual perception is extremely complex. Perhaps the issue we are concerned with is what in the cinema fixes (under the regime of repetition) meaning, perception and subjectivity—all of which have their own distinct and different historical momentums—and whether it is this fixing process we call pleasure. If cinema is historical, so is pleasure. If cinema is ideological, so is pleasure. Hence the question: Can pleasure be instrumentalized, institutionalized, used and abused, exploited, transformed, and made 'political'? It is therefore not enough to say, as economic historians of the cinema might, that the history of the cinema finds its place within the histories of the entertainment industry, because it is quite clear that concepts such as entertainment, leisure and culture are as much in need of further analysis as are the notions of pleasure and desire. Are the spectators of cinema, one must ask, prisoners of pleasure and desire in a world ruled by power and productivity? Is the question of cinema ultimately one about a power/pleasure nexus that is beginning to displace other, older dichotomies, like the relation history/subjectivity or the opposition work/ leisure?

The 'historiographical project,' then, has to address both sides of the power/pleasure configuration as well as the terms which are thereby subsumed. What needs to be noted, however, are the conditions that allow us now to conceive of such a project. The cinema has become a historical phenomenon, perhaps not quite in the sense that its beginning and end can be defined and described, but in the sense that the mutations and shifts now evident within the institution cinema and the institution pleasure are such that something forcibly detaches itself about the beginning of the cinema as well. From this perspective cinema does become historical, i.e., conditioned by specific and local circumstances. This is the challenge today; if we persist in sticking to the old questions, the cinema will appear as dead, offering no resistance to its appropriation by academics and film scholars.

It is true that in all the traditional areas of film history ('who did what, when and why') as well as in the relatively newer fields, such as the legal ramifications of the industry or the relations of technology to film style or genre, 'more work needs to be done.' But one cannot help feeling that most of this work will confirm and illustrate paradigms which are themselves in need of revision. If one fails to realize the extent to which our society's ideological tasks of visual representation, of narrative and iconography, of socialization and forms of address, of subject-positioning and consensus politics, have shifted from cinema to television and advertising, then questions concerning the 'spectator in the text,' or the coherence of the film-text and its relation to other 'texts,' will all become academic. For a film today is as much constructed 'outside'—in the discourses of financing and of spin-offs and residuals, in promotional campaigns and journalistic or critical reviews—as it is constructed within the length and duration of its celluloid strip and the space of its projection.

Such a situation has implications about the way one writes even about individual films. For they construct themselves as filmic texts and social texts simultaneously, and clearly the emphasis on the problems of 'representation'—as a theoretical and political issue—fully reflects such an awareness. On the other hand, to disregard the degree to which cinema audiences have become specialized in recent decades, or not to consider bingo halls at one extreme and video-game parlors at the other in relation to the traditional spaces and audiences of cinema, is to reduce questions about the historical spectator of the cinema to a mere manipulation of statistics. The manner in which the cinema today binds its audience with 'special effects,' 'fetishistic' representations of technology, of sexuality, of violence—the limit-cases of representation and perception (indicative of the cinema's current function as 'an institution whose chief concern is not the production of more or less acceptable representation but the crisis of representations')[10]—has repercussions on how one chooses to define and analyze the historical nature of spectatorship and pleasure.

In order to resituate the 'questions of cinema' (Stephen Heath's phrase), it has therefore become customary to center investigations of many traditional problems around the notion of spectatorship and pleasure and, in particular, to specify the cinema in terms of '*Schaulust*' (visual pleasure)—often connected with narrative, sexual difference and representation. But while this clarifies the notion of spectatorship by pointing to a structural connection between identification, projection, representation, narration and image, major difficulties still remain about the historical nature of this spectatorship. In addition, the almost invariably posited link between visual pleasure and narrative, while opening up crucial questions in relation to Hollywood and classical narrative, may not account for practices other than those of classical narrative, whether they are avant-garde alternatives or culturally specific variants of mainstream commercial cinema.

In attempting to historicize the questions of pleasure and spectatorship, one may have to be more radical and forego the notion of narrative as that which founds and anchors, regulates and defines, visual pleasure.[11] Too close an identification of visual pleasure with narrative leaves the argument within a concept of textual boundaries difficult to sustain in the light of the historical changes mentioned above. What needs to be opened up is how visual pleasure in the cinema relates to non-cinematic forms of visual pleasure, e.g., the very real difference between 'perversion' in a clinical sense and voyeurism or scopophilia in the cinema. And one would like to know more about *Schaulust* under other conditions of spectacle—such as concerts, shows, sports, parades, public occasions—where the questions of narrativity, sequencing and causality are quite different from those encountered in fictional narratives (unless our concept of narrative is considerably redefined).

Furthermore, if Christian Metz is right in thinking that visual pleasure attaches itself not to the object film but to the institution cinema, within which the object film becomes merely the activating instance of pleasure or unpleasure, the fetish or the object of boredom and disgust, then the question of how the discourses of cinema first tried to bind the spectator to the apparatus, before developing the discourses around the star or around familiar narratives, becomes once again obscured.[12] What would lose all historical specificity, in other words, is how the cinema engaged with narrative as a particular strategy of audience-orientation.[13] These are problems which film theory in recent years has attempted to address, notably by reinvestigating early cinema and the 'constitution of the codes,' to use Noël Burch's phrase. Burch in particular wants to focus critically on 'narrative' as the crucial historical variable. His work suggests that there is nothing in the cinematic apparatus as such, or indeed in visual pleasure, that predestines the cinema's massive turn to narrative.

Weimar Cinema and Film History

In these discussions, a special place is occupied by the German cinema of the silent period, or more accurately, that part of Germany's film production between 1913 and 1933 which has survived in archives or film history textbooks as either German Expressionist or German Realist cinema. This is not only because of the number of films that have become world cinema classics, or the importance of the directors who subsequently left Germany as *emigrés* and exiles to the United States, but also because technical innovation and advances, mainly in the fields of camera work, lighting and studio architecture, gave this German cinema an almost paradigmatic importance in the definition of film style, editing and *mise-en-scène* generally. Also, some typical examples, such as *The Cabinet of Dr. Caligari, Nosferatu* or *Dr. Mabuse the Gambler*, have been considered as key works of avant-garde cinema, whereas others, equally topical, such as *The Last Laugh, Madame Dubarry*, and *The Joyless Street*, had an appreciable influence on fixing the norms of the mainstream narrative cinema. Yet quite apart from this, and in apparent contradiction, German cinema of this period has served as a test case for traditional film histories and sociologies of the cinema, in particular those attempting to define the methodological status of concepts such as 'movement,' 'period' or 'national cinema'—problems that may now themselves seem historical, except insofar as they highlight textual systems, subject-effects and economic determinants different from those of classical Hollywood narrative cinema. At this level of generality, where film history seeks to establish a pertinent relation between stylistic or narrative characteristics on the one hand, and economic and social developments on the other, the German silent cinema has therefore been given a lot of attention. Whether analyzed by an art historian (Lotte Eisner), a social psychologist (Siegfried Kracauer) or more economically-oriented sociologists and historians (George Huaco, Andrew Tudor, Paul Monaco), a remarkable degree of homogeneity, coherence and even closure seems to typify this cinema.[14]

So why return to it now? There are two important reasons. First, it may be necessary to challenge the very closure and coherence with which the German cinema has been presented as demonstrating a relationship—however complex and in need of more refined understanding—between a given society and its cinema, between certain economic and political tendencies and currents in mass culture and modes of representation. It is true that there have been many general and particular criticisms of *From Caligari to Hitler* and *The Haunted Screen*. However, despite the fact that Kracauer's methodology especially continues to arouse harsh criticism, there has never been a serious challenge to the substance of these books: in Kracauer, the claim for a demonstrable relation between the films of Weimar and fascism, or in Eisner, the claim for a demonstrable relation between German Romanticism, Weimar films and fascism. This is due, I think, to the fact that although most film historians studiously avoid the 'national character' issue or a psycho-social reading of film texts, they still firmly hold to various forms of (mitigated) determinism. While perfectly willing to multiply the determinants of a given set of phenomena, in this instance the cinema, we are very reluctant to let go of some version of the 'final instance' or of positing some kind of 'conjunctural' model that would indicate how different events articulate themselves in different forms and at different levels but are nonetheless similarly structured and coextensive in space and time.

Geoffrey Nowell-Smith has outlined the dilemma very forcefully:

> We may take it as a starting point that cinema (or film) is immersed in a series of histories prior to its assuming any specific identity itself and therefore being capable of having a history of its own. These histories would be those of the economy, of technology, of politics and of ideology/representation—to which one might add the unconscious, which is itself ahistorical but meshes into the other histories in determinate ways. Each of these represents a level of determination which helps to fix the nature of the object cinema. . . . But cinema also has (or historically has acquired) its own specificity, insofar as its rise to be a mass art inaugurates a new apparatus that joins together the existing determinations in a new way.[15]

This statement balances the options very carefully: the cinema is the product of these various determinations, but, in turn, the product itself is capable of articulating the determinations in specific ways, and thus it acts as a determination in its own right. In the case of the Weimar period, Kracauer's book in many ways accomplishes just such a balancing act, because he is able to show different 'histories'—political, biographical, technological, industrial, economic and social—producing these films, but in order then to be able to suggest ways in which the films themselves crystallized, expressed or prepared a particular state of mind, which in turn became determining in the manner indicated by his title.[16] The argument against Kracauer is then merely one about the accuracy or exhaustiveness of the determinants and the specificity of the films, not about the nature of the interaction or the theoretical model.

It has in fact become the rule to speak, in the instance of such a non-linear but still interactive and causal model, of 'discourses' rather than determinants. This indicates the non-hierarchical aspect of the field, and emphasizes articulation and interpenetration as opposed to cause-and-effect chains or the old base-superstructure projection. In that case, the cinema would be one of the discourses (or a certain combination of several discourses) competing or interacting with other discourses and/or combinations of discourses within the social formation: other histories, other discourses—of institutions, of power, of pleasure, of knowledge, of sexuality, of representation, etc. It would then be simply a matter of choosing a particular vantage-point and unravelling articulations and intensities with a particular strategy in mind, say, that of pleasure and subject-positions.

But what if it turned out that the cinema was not the outcome of the histories of the optics, chemistry, technology and so forth that make up its 'apparatus' or its 'institutions'? Suppose instead that cinema was the beginning of the end of history, the apparatus that would contribute decisively to the suspension of history, just as the development of atomic weapons and atomic energy represents the suspension of certain conflicts rather than a new phase of historical struggles? Suppose that the very model is therefore in question, and the issue of specificity or influence, of a homology between films and a given society, of reflection or crystallization, cannot accurately seize the phenomenon because it still assumes an accumulative, additive, essentially positivist teleology (even if this teleology is expressed as a kind of circularity or dialectic where product 'X' is seized as both determined and determining). If this were so, we would instead have to conceive of a disjunctive change, or leap, where the appearance and semblance of identity and continuation conceal a radical non-identity and break. This would be not simply an inversion of determinations, but their termination. Here is where I see the second reason for returning to the Weimar cinema. If it can be shown that the most convincing case of a mutual determination between cinema and history—and I am taking Weimar cinema as such—cannot be sustained, then all the other applications of the model and its ramifications become in turn problematic. The first step, then, is to examine the insufficiencies of prevailing accounts of Weimar cinema; therefore, it is necessary to indicate in what ways the construction of the films, their textual systems, are irreducible to and resist the determinants that have been adduced.

'Classical Narrative' or Avant-garde?

As we increase our understanding about Hollywood cinema, its institutional forms, its narrative drives and its textual limits, we have become more sensitive and also more curious about 'alternative practices' within film history, both for their own sake, and as traditions or programs for avant-garde or independent cinema. Two areas have been investigated with particular care: the Japanese cinema, as offering a radically different conception of narrative space, and the 'pre-Griffith' American silent cinema. In one case, it is the question of another culture and the possibility of a different aesthetic of pictorial and dramatic representation; in the other, of an earlier, historically specific logic of narration within the same cultural and ideological space as classical narrative itself.

Noël Burch has identified himself with work on both these fronts. In his article on Edwin S. Porter, he has been at pains to establish Porter's films as ambivalent rather than transitional film texts, as standing at the intersection of two distinct modes of representation instead of exemplifying, as in most film histories, different stages of a linear process that goes from 'primitive' to 'mature.' For Burch, Porter becomes emblematic of two distinct possibilities of representation and signification in film, one of which has been suppressed, marginalized and all but forgotten by the other, dominant one that in effect went on to write film history on its own behalf. Discussing *Life of An American Fireman*, in the version deposited at the Library of Congress in 1903, Burch notes what in his view distinguishes Porter's film from 'classical narrative':

> The next shot shows the facade of the burning house. The woman appears at the window, makes an agitated appeal, and disappears. The firemen set up a ladder—and we see, obviously occupying the same length of time, the same action that we previously witnessed from inside the house.
>
> Seeing this curious document in the form in which I have described it . . . any historian worthy of the name ought to find the process of its 'dialectical' gestation obvious enough: sensing the as yet still distant possibility of absolute ubiquity in the camera—the possibility, that is to say, that the spectator might accept a series of shots as being different points of view of a single continuous action, rather than simply variants of 'what he might see from his seat' (here I am simplifying problems that are more complex)—Porter in fact films one action twice, from two different 'points of view' (actually the two were several miles apart, which also implies an extraordinary intuition of the possibilities offered by montage in the area of fictitious connections, theorized by Kuleshov some twenty years later). But at the same time Porter felt, probably with reason, that the audience was not yet ready to accept this sort of transportation in space-time, and he (or someone else, it doesn't really matter) decided to show the two actions successively—which obviously has the effect of undermining the already remarkably controlled sequential linearization of the preceding scenes. So once again one of Porter's 'steps forward' in fact ends by accentuating some features of the primitive cinema even more strongly than before: its non-homogeneity in *The Life of An American Cowboy*, its non-occlusion in *The Great Train Robbery*, and here its non-linearity.[17]

For Burch, classical narrative is defined by its articulation of space and time in terms of clearly ordered hierarchies, which force the spectator's eye to participate in a cinematic space constructed solely to accommodate perspectival vision and which place the perceiving subject as both center and origin of the representation, with a systematic elision of everything that does not contribute to enhancing the forward-moving flow.

Burch, I think, is quite right to speculate about the historical determinants that in the American cinema displaced a conception such as Porter's in favor of Griffithian forms of continuity editing, which break down scenes for purposes of sequential narrativization. But his (rough) distinctions between folk-art modes of representation and their proletarian roots as against bourgeois forms of narrative do not altogether convince, if only for lack of more specific evidence. It is precisely this question of further evidence that makes the Weimar cinema so interesting and important.

It seems to me that in respect of the articulation of time and space, of linear and non-linear narrative, the German silent cinema presents a textual system that is different from both Porter's kind of ambivalence and Griffith's or 'post-Griffithian' classical narrative, and yet is decidedly and significantly a 'bourgeois' cinema. What, then, are *its* determinants, or conversely, was this a formalist cinema which belonged to a yet to be constituted avant-garde? As I understand Burch, he has chosen in Porter a successful commercial director, undoubtedly in the mainstream of the narrative fiction film, so as to be able to posit some kind of historical determination for Porter's work. If one were to stay within the theoretical model and investigate in a systematic manner the films of the Weimar cinema, the same kinds of conclusions would result.

Pascal Bonitzer, in an article on Hitchcock and suspense, also talks about the distinction between 'primitive cinema' and classical narrative:

> This is the turning point represented by Griffith, the age of the close-up and montage. . . . What we here have is a cinematic revolution. With the arrival of montage, the close-up, immobile actors, the look (and its corollary—the banishment of histrionics) an entire facade of the cinema seems to disappear and be lost forever; in a word, all the excrement of vaudeville. The cinema was 'innocent' and 'dirty.' It was to become obsessional and fetishistic. The obscenity did not disappear, it was interiorized, moralized and passed into the register of desire. . . . As the body became more or less immobilized and the look was enthroned, morality, perversion and desire intervened for the first time in the cinema. . . . Such is the slant by which fiction makes its entry. For, as Godard has said in a recent book, and in precise reference to Hitchcock, it is the look which formulates the fiction.[18]

Bonitzer's is perhaps itself a 'classical' formulation of the origin of classical narrative within a psychoanalytically conceived film theory. For such a theory, Weimar cinema is of particular interest, because the look is in some sense consistently privileged. And in this respect, it also challenges the historical division between primitive and post-Griffithian cinema, since a film like *The Student of Prague* (1913) is entirely conceived within the ambit of the look and desire, yet its editing technique belongs to the pre-Griffith period.[19] It would be absurd, however, to call such a film 'primitive.' In it, as in Porter according to Burch, a mode of representation other than 'classical' is operative—and this characteristic can be found in much of the German cinema throughout the early 1920s. Burch seems to acknowledge the difficulty (and he compounds a possible misunderstanding) when in a footnote to his Porter article he characterizes *The Cabinet of Dr. Caligari* as being 'much closer to the primitives (or to us) than to Griffith or De Mille.'[20] The danger, it seems to me, is to see a film like *Caligari* as belonging to 'primitive' cinema, or of making it part of an avant-garde whose formal concerns are deemed to be exempt from historical determinations.

Yet it may well be the case that within a film history emerging out of psychoanalysis, based on a codification and hierarchization of the spectator's look (and the model of the psychic apparatus adduced to conceptualize it), such a practice as that exemplified by the German silent cinema cannot be accounted for 'historically.' Or rather, its historicity inscribes itself in the general history of the cinema, for a theorist like Burch, as emblematic of the possibility of a radically different—formalist, 'modernist'—practice of filmic signification. He has tried to make such an argument for the early films of Fritz Lang, but his 'propositions' presuppose a discontinuity so incisive that it does not allow us to account for the evident 'influence' the German silent cinema has itself had on classical Hollywood narrative and the whole tradition of *mise-en-scène*.[21]

Kracauer's analysis

The most thorough attempt at outlining the historical determinants of a body of films whose common denominator is neither author nor genre but a historical period—itself defined by what terminated it—is *From Caligari to Hitler*. In the present context it is worth noting that Kracauer sees the Weimar cinema as a narrative cinema—one that through its narratives works over a complex cultural heritage, which combines literary with folk-art motifs, and mass-culture stereotypes of visual iconography with more directly historical and ideological references. Kracauer supports his arguments primarily with plot synopses and the striking evidence of repeated motifs across seemingly distinct generic or authorial codes. This makes him posit a structural convergence between story and history, dramatic conflict and social conflict. He thus deduces a level of determination above or outside the individual texts, whose coherence can only be understood in the light of these extra-cinematic factors—although Kracauer is careful not to assume any kind of mono-causal, unilinear determining instance. History, for him, has to be seized at the phenomenal level, where agent and subject remain virtually anonymous, and intentionality or purpose manifest themselves almost by default while overtly pursuing other objectives. The cinema appears to him to be just such a field of fluid contours and seemingly indeterminate epiphenomena.[22]

It is against this philosophical and sociological background that one has to see the double process of abstraction that validates Kracauer's method of analogical reasoning: both German society and the films are constructed as narratives, and the characters' movements in the fiction become symbolic of the movements of classes, groups or historical subjects—constructions which he tries to name (not without irony) in terms such as 'the national character,' 'the German soul,' 'the collective mentality.' In other words, *From Caligari to Hitler* is itself built like a 'classical narrative,' a kind of Griffithian cross-cutting between the condensed super-fiction of a hundred-odd feature films and the political or sociological fortunes of the German people during the same period. What ensures the coherence and power of conviction in this construction, what anchors the various moments of social and fictional articulation, is a level of psychological truth and consistency, the psycho-critical analysis of a recognizable 'disposition' or character typology. It must be added, however, that Kracauer—like other Freudo-Marxist *emigrés* to the United States such as Erich Fromm—regarded the emphasis on psychological and emotional conflict in mass-cultural products itself as a typically bourgeois and petit-bourgeois displacement of political and social problems and anxieties.

Thus the types of narratives that characterize Weimar cinema, according to Kracauer, invariably involve the kind of triangulation of desire familiar from narratives we are now accustomed to calling 'oedipal':[23] violent rivalry between an older and a younger man over the same woman (*Variety, Pandora's Box*), where the rival might be different in class (*Student of Prague, Phantom*); he could be the father (*Pandora's Box, Metropolis*), or the woman's father (*Shattered*) jealous of a suitor. The 'father' might be fantasmatized into Death (*Destiny*), a vampire (Nosferatu), the Tsar or Harun-al-Rashid (*Waxworks*), or Jack the Ripper (*Waxworks, Pandora's Box*). He might be brother disguised as monk (*Schloss Vogeloed*), an enemy brother (*Chronicle of Grieshuus, The Brothers Schellenberg*), a cousin (*Secrets of a Soul*), the hero's double (*Student of Prague, The Other*), his moral opponent (*Dr. Mabuse the Gambler*) or his best friend (*The Cabinet of Dr. Caligari*). The common elements seem to be the protagonist's suicidal tendencies, the frequent representation of the other as monstrous, the repeated incest motif as explicit motivation and the horrifying but also petrifying and fascinating spectacle of manipulated abuses of power and authority. Pamela Falkenberg has summarized a certain dynamic in the patterns:

> One of the things we have noted about oedipal structures in the German films of the 20s and 30s is their peculiar instability, particularly the instability of the place of the father (for instance, in the analysis of *Dr. Mabuse*). Fathers are displaced and replaced, and those that are displaced reappear to reclaim their place (i.e., the sequel to *Dr. Mabuse*). And, even when more 'positive' father figures appear to take the place of ones which have been cast by the narrative as dangerous or destructive, these 'positive' figures, either overtly or covertly, tend to take on the

characteristics of the originally destructive figure (e.g., the supposedly kindly psychiatrist at the end of *Dr. Caligari*). . . . The position of the mother in these oedipal configurations is also peculiar. Father and son figures compete for her, but they are also ambivalent about her, and in some cases desire to eliminate her altogether (*The Last Laugh, The Blue Light*).[24]

These are also the features underlined by Kracauer's study, where Freudian personality traits and characterology serve as metaphors for a socio-political analysis. In this respect, the homosexual, paranoid, narcissistic fantasies which constitute Kracauer's portrait of the 'German soul' as masculine, masochistic and 'tossed between rebellion and submission' can certainly be read off the films with persuasive regularity, if it makes sense to grant the initial premise (of any sociology of film?), namely that:

> . . . the films of a nation reflect its mentality, . . . not so much as explicit credos as psychological dispositions—those deep layers of collective mentality which extend more or less below the dimension of consciousness.[25]

The merit of Kracauer's book is to have pointed to the systematic overcoding of oedipal situations across a wide variety of fictional and sociological referents. This effectively challenges a division between 'fantas-tic' and 'realistic' genres or tendencies, as well as the stylistic, art-historical distinctions between 'Expressionism' and '*Neue Sachlichkeit*' in the German cinema. On the other hand, the father-son conflicts and their resolutions in favor of the father are part of the standard *topoi* of expressionist literature and drama, to the extent of giving 'Weimar Germany' its overall identity in the minds of social and cultural historians. The rebellion that failed: in such a configuration the oedipal or generational conflict does double duty as a metaphor for the class struggle. Yet insofar as Kracauer, while sensitive to the metaphoric role of a psychoanalytic character typology in relation to social conflict, nonetheless tends to read the fictional protagonists as— metaphorically or metonymically symbolized—representations of conflicts that have their reality elsewhere, the question still remains about the narrative or narrational level at which one might assume these economic conflicts to manifest themselves. For, as Mary Ann Doane has pointed out, 'If class conflict is repressed by Weimar cinema (and there is every reason to believe this is the case), we can not expect it to be explicitly linked with character typology.'[26]

Paradoxically, given the literary, Lukácsian echoes of his theory of reflection, Kracauer is most conclusive in his interpretations whenever the films are evidently non-realistic, i.e., 'Gothic,' and where it is by no means easy to point to a stable narrative structure that could support a symbolic reading. In fact, the desire to see the films as elaborating analogies with social and national history means that Kracauer has to fill gaps, smooth out the narrative logic, invert the causal chains, level off intensities, and thereby deny or put aside the very resistances and ambiguities that make these films different from realist-illusionist narrative. In other words, the *forces* of stylization, excess, displacement and repression which so evidently mark the textual systems never come into view or are analyzed in Kracauer's interpretation. Two alternative responses to such a critique appear possible: either Kracauer's analysis of narrative has to be supplemented by an argument that makes evident the particular relationship between narration, subject position and visual pleasure/visual anxiety as it characterizes the different film texts of Murnau, Lang, Pabst and others; or the specific textual effects of the Weimar cinema have to be seen in a context other than that of visual pleasure and narrative altogether.

In the first case, one would be looking for a theory that was attentive to the many levels of narrative ambiguity, especially those created by editing and point-of-view, in films like *Nosferatu* and *The Last Laugh*, but also *The Cabinet of Dr. Caligari* and *Dr. Mabuse the Gambler*, as well as lesser-known films such as *Shattered* or *Warning Shadows*. In a seminar on the subject of precisely this narrative ambiguity and reversibility in Weimar cinema, the concept that appeared most useful in accounting for the intensities and elisions of the textual systems of these films was that of 'The Uncanny' as introduced by Freud, but also in the way it had been reformulated for literary theory by Samuel Weber:

> Uncanny is a certain indecidability which affects and infects representations, motifs, themes, and situations. . . . But the uncanny is not merely identical with this indecidability: it involves and implies a second moment or movement, namely the defense against this crisis of perception and phenomenality, a defense which is ambivalent and expresses itself in the compulsive curiosity . . . the craving to penetrate, discover and ultimately to conserve the integrity of perception: perceiver and perceived, the wholeness of the body, the power of vision—all this implies a denial of that almost-nothing which can hardly be seen, a denial that in turn involves a certain structure of narration, in which this denial repeats and articulates itself.[27]

This passage clearly links perception and the gaze with narrative and narration. The fantastic themes, the heavy borrowing of literary motifs from Romanticism, which has helped to perpetuate the misleading label 'Expressionist cinema,' could be brought into relation with a cinematic practice that consistently constructed the profilmic space in accordance with the characters' subjectivity, which in itself is almost entirely organized around the gaze, around perception and effects of editing that interiorize and subjectify the reading of the image. Hence it becomes possible for Doane to write that:

The strategy through which the Weimar cinema confronts the gaze—a strategy of simultaneous appropriation as representation and implementation as a formal means of structuration—is also the strategy through which it confronts the notion of the Double and the concept of doubling or repetition.[28]

The outcome of such a conceptualization is that *mise-en-scène* is no longer the expression of a stylistic will, be it that of an individual director or a like-minded group or movement ('Expressionism'), but finds its function in the now familiar idea of the cinema 'constituting or placing the subject in representation,' 'getting the spectator into the picture.' Psychoanalytical film theory has helped to define the cinematic imaginary of classical narratives as one primarily revolving around (male) narcissism and castration anxiety. These notions seem entirely compatible with the concept of the Uncanny, the emphasis on specularity, and the commonly held views of the social character of Weimar Germany.[29] In the context of the films in question, one might be more specific:

Narcissism remains a significant element of the uncanny because 'narcissism is both the precondition of and in part the reaction to the castration complex.' Narcissism is a *defensive* reaction to the possibility of castration and therefore, although the 'uncanny is bound up with a *crisis* of perception and phenomenality,' it also entails a protection against that crisis. . . . This denial of the 'crisis of perception and phenomenality' (which the notion of castration entails) is consistently re-articulated through the narrational structure of the Weimar films. This can be seen not only in the use of the self-contained frame, glance/object editing and the consequent desire for a unity, simultaneity and coherence of vision, but in the very lack of distance between narrative and narration. The framing devices and the use of texts simply establish a false origin or authority for the text—the narrative as a whole remains unqualified.[30]

This last point of Doane's, however, may give rise to some controversy. Her position would see the Weimar cinema as not fundamentally different from classical narrative, and thus merely a further instance of the generalized (Metzian) cinematic imaginary—historically specific only insofar as it exemplified the essentially bourgeois, patriarchal character of cinematic narrative. For this view the different narrational strategies do not fundamentally alter the subject-positions available to the spectator, and therefore do not give a sociologically or nationally specific structure to the articulation of visual pleasure and sexual difference—the very indices which in psychoanalytic film theory define 'classical narrative.' The determinations are those of the institution cinema as an apparatus that 'manages' to varying degrees the repression and disavowal of the male spectator's castration anxiety.

Kracauer's historical and sociological analysis of the 'German character' and the 'national disposition' in terms of petit-bourgeois masochism would thus appear as a phallocentric version of politics and history, which, when deconstructed, speaks its truth not so much about Germany or fascism, but—involuntarily—about the obsessional, fetishistic nature of 'classical narrative.' This is a position Patricia Mellencamp argues with polemical wit in an article on Fritz Lang's *Metropolis*:

> *From Caligari to Hitler* consistently and repetitiously depicts for over 270 pages a national, middle-class, oedipal/familial failure peculiar to Germany and its cinema, a failure which resulted in Hitler and World War II. Beneath its sociological pretense is a perverse discourse on sexuality (a staging of the repression thesis) which documents Foucault's thesis that from the mid-18th century on sexual discourse is 'historically bourgeois . . . in its successive shifts and transpositions, it induces specific class effects.' . . . Kracauer presents *his* thesis, *his* reading of German culture and politics through films as 'reflections' of social problems due to their popular status. In this analysis, there was 'something unaccountable in the domestic situation, not within the normal field of vision.' Granted that his reading is abnormal, the argument places the blame on the domestic family, or historically, patriarchy. What is not in psychoanalysis' 'field of vision' as well as Kracauer's, except in absence or negative opposition, was female sexuality, the figure of woman, woman's sex. In one sense, Kracauer argues a massive failure of the family to properly inscribe males into the symbolic of paternal order. . . . Kracauer dramatizes Foucault's thesis: he constantly speaks about sex while maintaining it as the secret through which every individual must pass in order to gain access to the proper construction of the social body. (Because this text speaks for itself, I feel little 'compulsion' to analyze its position; clearly there are no secrets of reading involved, no concealed structures that must be brought to the surface. Neither amassed empirical facts nor his many thematic interpretations can conceal or contain the symptoms of male hysteria.)[31]

The metaphor of the 'field of vision' may indeed be the crucial one: it refers us back not only to the specifically cinematic, but also to the relation between perception and psychoanalysis which investigations of the Uncanny attempt to clarify. But if it is true that castration anxiety is that which is pointed to as the pivotal structure of the texts, and that the films of the Weimar cinema share with their severest critic, i.e., Kracauer, the same 'male hysteria,' then it is clear that the differences between Weimar cinema and 'classical Hollywood narrative' are indeed insignificant, compared to the massive displacement and hysterical articulation of female sexuality that they have in common. The question, then, becomes rather one of deciding how it is possible that certain films nonetheless allow the female spectator to assume a pleasurable subject-position.[32] To generalize from her analysis of *Metropolis*, Mellencamp is no more prepared than Kracauer to see in some films a degree of ambiguity and indecidability that would allow the female spectator to appropriate them for the construction of *her* visual pleasure. Both Kracauer's reading of the narratives and Mellencamp's deconstruction of his argument from a feminist perspective depend on enclosing the texts in a series of (negative) determinations, in the light of which the particularly filmic effects of the Weimar cinema can no longer be valorized. Yet, in German silent films the authority, origin and control of the act of narration was constantly foregrounded, and in a manner that had no equivalent in contemporary silent cinema of other countries. The profusion of nested narratives, framed tales, flashbacks, *en-abîme* constructions and interlacing of narrative voices emerges as the index of the very difference that singled out German silent cinema as historically specific.

The Historical Spectator

The German historical/hysterical male has actually been the subject of a number of studies, from Wilhelm Reich's *Mass Psychology of Fascism* and certain sections of Adorno's *Authoritarian Personality* to a recent West German study of the sexual fantasies among the *Freikorps* (a right-wing para-military organization in the 1920s) as documented in the literary and sub-literary publications by and for their members.[33] These studies do pay much attention to the relationship between class and economic status on the one hand, and psychological or sexual dispositions on the other. Kracauer's book could well be seen within this context, notably where he asks himself how psychological factors could become as important as they did in the Fascists' rise to power, given a fairly homogeneous class ideology among urban populations, based on their 'pretensions' and aspirations rather than their actual class positions.

The answer may well be that there is indeed for the German spectator of the 1920s a social and economic dimension to castration anxiety and the Uncanny. For what the middle-class and petit-bourgeois family lived in fear of was loss of social status:

> The behavior of broad middle-class strata also seemed to be determined by overwhelming compulsions. In a study published in 1930 I pointed out the pronounced 'white-collar' pretensions of the bulk of German employees, whose economic and social status in reality bordered on that of the workers, or was even inferior to it. Although these lower middle-class people could no longer hope for bourgeois security, they scorned all doctrines and ideals more in harmony with their plight, maintaining attitudes that had lost any basis in reality.[34]

The structure that Kracauer is here outlining indicates behavior that involves both disavowal and identification with an Other, although what is being identified with and simultaneously feared is class difference. This may explain why there are so many films of the Weimar cinema where a 'gothic' or 'uncanny' motif is introduced to cover up a potential class difference, notably *Nosferatu* and *Phantom* but also *The Cabinet of Dr. Caligari*, where the medium's first victim is the town official who treats the doctor as if he belonged to the *Lumpenproletariat*.[35] In *Metropolis*, the disavowal of sexual difference (exemplified in the two Marias) becomes the symbolic structure that allows the disavowal of class difference to appear as 'resolution.' One can, however, go further and, with Richard de Cordova, see the very narrative structures themselves as part of the same textual strategy:

> We have, to this point, seen the framed tale (through the structure of castration-anxiety) referring itself as a disavowal through which the ego-libido remains intact. It may now be possible to propose there is a corollary paranoiac structure through which 'apparent' aggressivity is projected from the ego-libido to the object-libido. This paranoiac structure would necessarily be a secondary projection emanating from the former, narcissistic one. In *The Last Laugh*, aggressivity is directed towards the middle class . . . it is subverted though, by its designation as the 'unreal' part of the story. This raises the question: 'Whose secondary projection are we witnessing?' . . . As we have seen [the framing devices mean] that it cannot be attributed to [the characters in the fiction]. It can only be attributed to the spectator inscribed within the text, or in a broader sense, to the audiences of the day as they were subjected to this inscription. There is a particular over-determination of libidinal placement (anxiety/aggressivity). . . . If aggressivity is discharged where the stability of the entire system (social, psychological, filmic) is threatened, then it follows that aggressivity interpellates the subject within an unstable but specifiable type of object relation. . . . The textual interaction of narcissism and paranoia articulated in the Weimar films obviates the possibility of seeing these films as any kind of direct reflection of the society in which they were made. A historical spectator was inscribed within these texts and ascribed a particular imaginary position within their symbolic functioning.[36]

What evidence do we have that might further substantiate the idea that 'a historical spectator was inscribed within these texts'? When one reads *From Caligari to Hitler*, one is often baffled to find the films criticized as much for what they omit as for what they say, while it is never clear whether the political symbolism and sinister forebodings are given a locus of intentionality or whether the *Zeitgeist* envelops the film industry, the director and the spectator all in one. This, as I tried to suggest, is due to the fact that Kracauer's argument is decentered. Not only do the forces generating the structures of which the films are symptoms never come into view, but the critical position from which Kracauer conducts his investigation is equally veiled. An essay by Kracauer written in 1928, 'Shopgirls at the Movies,' defines the problem much more sharply:

> Films are the mirror of our present society. They are made with the financial means of corporations, which, in order to realize their profits, have to hit the taste of the public at all cost. Never will a producer be seduced into presenting subjects that attack the basis of society in the slightest; he would undermine his own existence as a capitalist entrepreneur. . . . In order to investigate contemporary society, one would have to ask the products of the film industry into the confessional. They all blurt out an indelicate secret, without really wanting to. In an infinite series of films a limited number of typical motifs recurs time and again; they indicate how society wants to see itself represented. The essence of the filmic motifs is at the same time the sum of the reigning ideologies, which an interpretation of these motifs can demystify.[37]

The passage makes clear Kracauer's own intellectual position before he left for the United States. He was a writer of anti-capitalist critiques of the mass media which were very close to, and in fact a significant influence on, Horkheimer and Adorno's critical theory of the 'Culture Industry.' Shorn of its economic analysis, Kracauer's thesis in *From Caligari to Hitler* becomes something approximating a tautological, self-fulfilling conspiracy theory. That the reasons for this lack have to be sought in United States anti-communism after World War II becomes clear from Kracauer's correspondence with his publisher and the curiously ingratiating preface:

> I have reason to believe that the use made here of films . . . can profitably be extended to studies of current mass-behavior in the U.S. . . . studies of this kind may help in the planning of films . . . which will effectively implement the cultural aims of the U.N.[38]

The second important aspect of Kracauer's 1928 essay is its precise formulation of a theory of identification and self-recognition in the cinema. It is the non-realistic genres, texts of repression, displacement and decenteredness, that bind the spectator affectively to representation:

> In reality, it may be a rare occurrence that a cleaning lady marries the owner of a Rolls Royce; but is it not the dream of the Rolls Royce owner to make the cleaning ladies dream of aspiring to his level?[39]

Fairy tale motifs and uncanny moments may in fact be the dominant ways in which the spectator can recognize and organize his/her experience of reality in fictional form, which is nothing less than to argue that the only mode of identification in the mass media under capitalism is necessarily a form of self-alienation, even if the spectator is unaware that he/she can only recognize or respond to subjectivity in 'alienated' representations. What Kracauer does not stress is the degree to which editing and point-of-view, as well as 'filmic motifs,' construct the triangulation of identity that governs the mutually confirming self-images of 'Rolls Royce owner' and 'cleaning lady.'

The prototype of Kracauer's spectator in *From Caligari to Hitler*, his historical subject, is the petit-bourgeois white-collar worker—a sociological phenomenon in Germany only since the vast expansion of the bureaucratic apparatus following on unification in 1871, when Berlin became the capital of the *Reich*. This army of employees in the various new service industries was ideologically very volatile and divided (drawn from the rural *Hinterland* of Berlin into the swelling metropolis), yet its appearance became politically important only after the (brief) economic boom and recovery around the mid-1920s. Though its members did not possess a distinct class-consciousness of their own, their economic existence was such that they were thoroughly motivated by bourgeois ambitions while living in constant fear of being proletarianized. Traumatized by inflation and the specter of unemployment, their 'psychological disposition' (Kracauer) in the late 1920s may indeed have borne the imprint of their social condition and economic precariousness.

Kracauer described this new 'class,' its work habits, public behavior, leisure pursuits and family structures, in a seminal study entitled *Die Angestellten*, published in 1930. The phenomenological approach of this analysis owes much to Georg Simmel, but in its method it not only anticipates the countless sociological studies of the 1940s and 1950s in the United States (Lazarsfeld, Riesman, C. Wright Mills, *et al.*), but also embodies Kracauer's own model when he came to write *From Caligari to Hitler* in the 1940s. This means that Kracauer took the type of mass audience of the cinema from around 1928 and projected it backwards to the very beginning of the German cinema. A problem, however, is that the two crucial periods he identifies in *From Caligari to Hitler* (1913–15, 1919–23) actually indicate a somewhat different target-audience and constituency. As can easily be shown, the 'classic' German cinema (or 'Expressionist cinema') is a self-conscious attempt at bourgeois cinema, and the issue we are here concerned with, namely to account for the 'stylistic' and textual differences of this cinema from classical Hollywood narrative, has to take account precisely of this self-consciously 'artistic' impulse behind the films. When one looks at the cinema of the late 1920s in Germany, one cannot but become aware of a certain assimilation of Hollywood norms in comparison to the earlier periods, if only in terms of a superficial mark—the attenuation of psychological-fantastic motifs in favor of greater sociological 'realism.'

Kracauer's 'national character' and 'German soul' can thus, with some justification, be historicized and specified as the mass audience of the late 1920s—the sociopolitical group that, traditionally, has been seen to be most easily prone to and seduced by a fascist ideology. But if this was not the primary audience of the 'classical' German film, then the sweeping teleology of Kracauer's argument suffers equally from distortions and generalizations. What is elided is, in particular, a more differentiated awareness of modes of ideological and psychological self-recognition and self-estrangement—the kind of awareness Kracauer did in fact demonstrate in 'Shopgirls at the Movies.' We know from other empirical studies done in Hollywood in the 1930s that identification differs among spectators according to class, sex and age.[40] The history of the German cinema may well be characterized by the various attempts on the part of producers to find fictional and narrative forms in which the predominant audience of the day recognized itself ideologically (i.e., in its class- or sex-specific imaginary) but, at the same time, to balance this priority with another one, namely retaining and increasing the industry's competitive position *vis-à-vis* Hollywood on the European market, which necessitated product differentiation and the creation of an 'art film' genre rich in production values.

The opposition between 'realism' and 'fantasy' that has traditionally served historians as a classification of the German silent cinema could indicate different modes of an overall objective: to bind heterogeneous audiences to the institution 'cinema.' It seems to me a mistake to assume that the cinema was from the beginning 'ideological' in the accepted sense. On the contrary, I believe that it is the task of film history to clarify the points and circumstances under which the cinema was appropriated as an instrument of ideology. The ideological symptomatology that underpins Kracauer's book is itself extremely contradictory. On the one hand, he wants to answer the historical and sociological question of how to explain the mass allegiance of 'the German people' to fascism, for as he says, 'behind the overt history of economic shifts . . . runs a secret history involving the inner dispositions.'[41] And in this interpretive explanatory project (whose object is social history, not film history), 'the medium of the German screen' becomes a social text— one among many—interacting with other discourses. On the other hand, precisely because Kracauer recognized the importance of the mass media as producers as well as bearers of ideology, the social text of the cinema is in some sense privileged, although not the final or even determining instance in the production of fascist ideology.

One might rephrase the dilemma by saying that Kracauer discovered both a historical problem and a theoretical one. The historical question has to do with the objects, discourses and fantasies that 'bind' a mass public to institutions and their orders of representation. Under this aspect, allegiance to the cinema and allegiance to Hitler become structurally related.[42] The theoretical question has to do with the definition of this structure, and here Kracauer does take his cue from Freud's work on identity as a structure of identification, projection, disavowal, castration anxiety and narcissism. This structure can indeed be studied with particular force in the films of the Weimar cinema, but the ideological determination, the historical content (so to speak) of this specifically cinematic structure of identification, may in the German cinema have been much more uncertain and complex than even Kracauer is willing or able to admit, because the book, at least at the outset, considers the cinema as its 'medium' rather than its object. In other words, the historical spectator of Kracauer and the 'textual' spectator of cinematic identification may not be identical. What is paradigmatic about the Weimar cinema is the structure of identification it represented and narrativized; what may be historical and historically specific are the reasons why it represented and narrativized cinematic identification at all.[43]

Freud's account of the construction of personal identity and identification operates within the confines of the bourgeois family. The Weimar cinema uses the family and oedipal conflicts as metaphors to dramatize fascination, the act of seeing, the obsession with the gaze—in short, the specularity and specularization of the visible world. Hence the ambiguity that characterizes the German cinema: What serves as the metaphor for what, and does it still make sense to ask this question? Is the family specularized, or is the spectacle that which subverts, challenges and disrupts the family?[44] In the American cinema, the pressures of motion picture production and financial investment made the cinema ideological much earlier, in the sense that it built itself around the maximization of audiences, disguising its own conditions and contradictions of existence. In Germany, this adaptation to the ideology of the spectator was a more complex process.

The 'Authors' Film

One of the reasons this process of ideological appropriation of the cinema as a stabilizing, 'binding' social force was not a smooth one can be located in the German intellectuals and members of the cultured bourgeoisie, who acted as the opinion-makers and supplied the critics working for the daily press, journals and reviews. They proved vociferously hostile to the cinema, especially in the years 1910–1914, the very years that saw the emergence of not only the German film industry, but also the type of film we are concerned with—the '*Autorenfilm*.' This debate about the cultural status of the cinema renewed itself in Germany (as in other European countries) periodically until the mid-1920s. The '*Kino-Debatte*' gives valuable clues to the specific forms of mediation—cinematic and non-cinematic—that were engaged in making the cinema respectable culturally and socially.[45] The *Autorenfilm* is a direct response, an intervention in the debates, as is *The Cabinet of Dr. Caligari*. One of the main points in the argument was an opposition to realism, strongly condemned by bourgeois critics as low and inartistic, because it presented *'Stoff'* (material) not 'worked over' by the shaping intelligence of the 'artist.' *The Cabinet of Dr. Caligari* was intended to prove that the cinema did not necessarily have to be a low mimetic form.[46]

The films that have survived as the 'classics' of the period are too diverse to fit a description that would make them mere by-products of an intellectual debate and a discussion of aesthetic theory. Such a claim would be historical determinism with a vengeance. On the other hand, it is important to be aware of instances of mediation, of discourses and forms of ideological coherence, which only detailed historical research can reconstruct. For instance, it is surprising to find how many films, especially in the early 1920s, were produced to coincide with the opening of new picture palaces in Berlin. This points not only to the relation between real estate and film production, but also to how carefully a specifically bourgeois audience was solicited in metropolitan Berlin. Renowned critics would be invited to speak before the film, and the ambiance was that of an important theatrical opening. By the late 1920s, press and advertising campaigns had been perfected, especially for a *'Grossfilm,'* so that the press book for *Metropolis* (1926), for example, gives valuable clues to marketing strategies and envisaged audience appeal. Indeed, Fritz Lang's interviews and essays in the quality monthlies and weekly press throughout his German career were always conscious of what cultural prejudices he had to flatter in order to subvert. At the same time, the evidence that is becoming available about planning and pre-production of a film like *Metropolis* suggests that its expensive special effects work and other production values were undertaken also to allow UFA to invest massively in new filmmaking technology, with the purposes of making the film suitable for U.S. export and of bringing the infrastructure in line with that of UFA's potential or actual competitors.

The fact that the films did, at the same time, form part of a theoretical-cultural debate not only reinforces the sense of an 'art cinema,' but indicates something else about the German film industry of the time. Precisely because a large slice of the 'commercial' market was firmly in the hands of at first French films and then (from 1919) Hollywood product, the German film industry's policy of product differentiation was deliberately aimed at capturing a 'minority audience' whose importance was its crucial role in the transmission of cultural values and aesthetic judgement.[47] Furthermore, it was only under economic conditions where many producers were supplying a still diffuse market that the Weimar cinema developed such a strong 'authors cinema,' for while UFA controlled distribution, it was by no means as monolithic in its production. Among the one hundred-odd production companies existing throughout the 1920s, both inside UFA and outside, one finds a deliberate policy towards the ambitious art film and stylistic experiment. Thus, the semblance of coherence for German films of the period, reproduced by scholars and critics, is in some sense one that the industry itself fostered as part of a marketing strategy, which included the launching of 'international' stars (such as Emil Jannings, Asta Nielsen, Pola Negri, Werner Krauss) and individually authored art films (such as those of Paul Wegener, Fritz Lang, F.W. Murnau).

Why difference should, however, manifest itself textually on the level of editing, composition, use of decor, lighting, acting and narrative construction is a question which can hardly be answered in economic terms. What has come to be known as *mise-en-scène*, and is commonly held to be the legacy of German silent cinema to classical narrative, also resists the type of explanation offered by Lotte Eisner.[48] Just as *The Cabinet of Dr. Caligari* quotes expressionist decor and acting rather than embodying it as an authentic style, what seems at issue in the diversity of stylistic idioms evident in the films (ranging from Gothic through Biedermeier, Orientalism, Neo-Romanticism, Jugendstil, Art-Deco and even Constructivism) is the very concept of an authentic or necessary style—so crucial to art history—as applied to the cinema. The often noted theatrical influence of Max Reinhardt is undeniable in the biographical context of many directors and actors. But it does not seem to account for the drastic changes that cinematic *mise-en-scène* had brought to the articulation of time and space and thus to the ambiguous interplay of action-time and narrated time, characteristic of the German silent cinema but quite alien to Reinhardt's theater. Also, it would seem that the determinants of the *mise-en-scène* and the textual systems of German cinema cannot be approached solely via a spectator-based film history, even if we historicize Kracauer's categories by distinguishing between a petit-bourgeois 'white collar' audience in the middle and late 1920s and a petit-bourgeois 'art-cinema' audience for the teens and the early 20s. If one analyzes films of the Weimar period in comparison to Nazi films, what is striking is the very instability, the excess and the self-conscious foregrounding of specular relations (voyeurism, visual pleasure, visual anxiety) in the textual systems and the narratives. By contrast, after 1933—partly owing to the coming of sound, but not decisively (as can be seen by three such typical 'Weimar' sound films as *Die Dreigroschenoper, M, Der Blaue Engel*)—all traces of this particular specularity in the *mise-en-scène* are eliminated, and the films appear readable in terms of classical narrative in much the same way as do Hollywood films of the 1930s. As a historian puts it:

> The political cult [i.e., Nazi/public spectacles and rituals] . . . called itself the true self-representation of the people. But the Nazi mass meetings as we see them in films or pictures today have lost their force: the flames on the sides of the Nuremberg stadium, the huge overwhelming flags, the marches and speaking choruses, present a spectacle to modern audiences not unlike those American musicals of the 1920s and

1930s which Hitler himself was so fond of watching each evening. It was not always so. For participants it was the symbolic content . . . that was so crucial to their sense of belonging.[49]

Indeed, the parallels between the American musical and the Nazi parades are significant in another respect, insofar as they are proof that fascination, voyeurism, identification and spectacle were, during the Nazi period, directly fetishized and libidinally fixed in the streets through parades, rallies and public speeches. Nazi cinema, on the other hand, shows a tendency to repress this voyeurism by a kind of functionalization and rationalization of the *mise-en-scène* and of editing. Here is a recent film-historical analysis:

> In the geometrical-hierarchical line-ups [of the Nazi Revue-film] not only the lack of discipline but also the fear of chaos finds itself bridled. When the 'girls' in, say, *We Dance Around the World* goose-step down the stairs in a pose of victorious triumph that takes them every night from Lisbon to Genoa, from London to Copenhagen, they are already crushing under their patent-leather boots anticipated uprisings. This is in-service dancing; some 'ride for Germany,' others dance and demonstrate in the sphere of entertainment a form which will find its expression in war.[50]

In this respect, the Weimar cinema appears as a transitional cinematic practice, the investigation of which has to proceed in the manner of a kind of archeology.

Two Types of Imaginary

Consideration of Kracauer and his analysis of the German audience have indicated that the social imaginary of Weimar cinema cannot be defined by a characterological portrait of the historical spectator. But what is clear is that the Weimar cinema posits the question of the relationship of visual pleasure and narrative cinema in ways different from the American cinema in two respects. First, visual pleasure appears inseparable from anxiety and is inscribed in a network of power and loss of power, control and loss of control. The text represses the protagonists' awareness of class difference and its seemingly insuperable nature. This scenario, this *mise-en-scène* of power and loss of control to which the protagonist is exposed raises the question of how the 'male' spectator can construct a pleasurable relation to these films.

Secondly, Kracauer seems to assume that the spectator feels the same masochism as the hero, which is in turn to assume direct identification. But this does not take account of what is perhaps the distinguishing feature of the Weimar cinema, namely its valorization of vision and the look evidenced in its emphasis on the act of seeing and being seen, its use of the point-of-view shot. For what is obvious is that this *mise-en-scène* of the look fundamentally alters the relationship of spectator to film and thus the question of identification. In other words, just as it is not possible to see the class conflicts present in and represented by the characters as a character typology, so the valorization of vision would fundamentally seem to transform the perception of anxiety into a pleasurable experience. This can only mean that the emphasis on vision allows the spectator some measure of control. Split in the process of representation, he is in fact watching himself, is in the position of the double. Out of control in the fiction, he is subject to another gaze; however, this other gaze is one that the spectator is not only subject to but also controls. The question of the historical spectator thus has to be rearticulated in terms of the indirection that comes, on the one hand, from foregrounding vision (or narration over action), and, on the other, from editing, the power of the look that is the camera's.

A closer analysis of individual films would be needed to detail what is meant by 'foregrounding vision.' What can be said, in light of the general views presented here, is perhaps only to point out how often the look motivates the narrative (the act of narration, by way of the cut on the glance) in films as dissimilar as *Madame Dubarry* and *The Nibelungen, Phantom* and *Pandora's Box.* The resulting relationships among the characters within the fiction, as well as the organization of off-screen space which mobilizes the spectators' powers of (inner) vision, crucially modify narrative continuity, the attributions of causality and agency, the articulation of space and time. Above all, this emphasis changes how one chooses to read the symbolic structure of the narrative, and thus how one interprets the oedipal positions that are being allocated to the characters by the fiction. In the Weimar cinema, the gaze is codified explicitly and implicitly as something that can substitute itself for other forms of power relations, in particular those normally associated with physical violence (of which there is practically none) and sexual stereotyping (rendered ambiguous by the instability of the male protagonists' sexual and social identity). But it also signifies more directly the power-nexus of the cinematic spectacle itself—modes of surveillance, manipulation, suggestibility, instrumentalization and 'object-hood.'

There is, however, a reason that one might want to go beyond specific cases and individual film texts. These textual effects relate to another 'crisis of perception,' outside the cinema, described this time not within psychoanalysis and film theory, but in Georg Lukács' account of 'reification'[51] as well as Walter Benjamin's remarks about shock-effects, visual stimuli, urbanization and the formation of the unconscious, perception, memory and experience:

> The greater the share of the shock factor in particular impressions, the more constantly consciousness has to be alert as a screen against stimuli; the more efficiently it does so the less do these impressions enter

Erfahrung, tending to remain in the sphere of a certain hour of one's life (*Erlebnis*).[52]

It is not possible here to explore the full implications of Benjamin's or Lukács' observations about the historical nature of human perception, visual decoding, attention span and memory. But it is important to note that they suggest a connection between specific forms of industrial organization, technological modes of production, demographic changes and urbanization on the one hand, and the emphasis that our society places on vision and the eye for the mastery and control of our everyday environment on the other. Similar work, such as that on the interdependence of the experience of time and space, the introduction of railways and timetables, and the synchroniza-tion of clocks and communication networks in the middle and late 19th century, indicates that a shift occurred as the transfer of sense experience from the proximity senses (touch, taste, smell) to those that control experience through distance (sight, hearing).[53] This cultural shift was, to a considerable extent, taken in charge by the cinema through its systematic over-development of voyeurism and scopophilia. The cinema's historical and ideological task would then have inscribed itself in an ensemble of discourses and social practices that translated particular forms of industrial organization and the mastery of space and time into a sensory perceptual discourse. Its effect has been to restructure both subjectivity and signification in the light of changes that capitalism has brought to all social relations. In this sense, not only the Weimar cinema, but all the cinematic institutions with which we are familiar may be called transitional phenomena, insofar as their social functions can be taken over and modified by other forms of visual and auditory pleasure. In the case of Germany, the history of its cinema would have to be extended not only by considering the specular organization of everyday public life as politics took to the streets and a dictatorship celebrated itself visually through endless pageants and parades, but also by assessing the role that, for instance, radio played in Hitler's war effort and the home front.[54]

The Weimar cinema may be called a transitional phenomenon for a more precise reason, one revolving around the very existence of a strong authors' cinema, and the economic as well as ideological conditions that made it possible for Germany to develop a film industry which, for a certain period, included a prestigious thriving sector not primarily or exclusively oriented towards a mass audience. For this line of inquiry, one might again turn to Burch, specifically his suggestion that, from the invention of the cinema onwards, two diametrically opposed tendencies found their imaginary expression in the cinema. These tendencies he locates neither in the needs of the spectators nor in the traditional stylistic opposition between 'realism' and 'fantasy,' but in the obsessions, drives and impulses of the inventors, mechanics and engineers who experimented with and constructed the cinema, who brought together the elements that came to constitute the 'cinematic apparatus.' In his book on Japanese cinema, Burch makes a distinction between 'breaking down human . . . movement' (the 'scientistic' motivation of Marey and Muybridge) and the drive towards 'synthesizing movement' (e.g., Edison's ambitions towards the 'Gesamtkunstwerk,' the synchronization of movement and sound).[55] This division, if it could be given more historical ground, might provide the basis for conceiving of another kind of imaginary, not that of the spectator but of the 'author.' On this level the 'author' would now be understood not in the narrow, traditional terms of the so-called 'auteur theory,' but as encompassing inventors, technicians, engineers, producers, directors—in short, all those who experience the fascination for the apparatus and the effects it can produce outside of and apart from the need to bind a given mass audience ideologically and psychically to acts of filmic consumption. In other words, this is an imaginary that in the first instance has less to do with the realism/pleasure/narrative nexus of popular culture and mass entertainment, and more to do with the capability of the Uncanny of film technology to produce its own 'imitation of life.'

It is not surprising that Burch, who as a theorist and film historian has supported the filmmakers of the avant-garde and is relentlessly hostile to the commercial cinema, should be particularly sensitive to the imaginary of the cinematic *bricoleur*.[56] A veritable definition of the avant-garde might be as a sector of filmmaking whose primary concern is with the exploration of the material and imaginary relation which binds the *filmmaker* to the filmic apparatus and for which the sociological impact of the medium (its institutional side/site) is secondary. This seems to me to offer not only an interesting possibility for reinvestigating the notion of the 'author,' but also for understanding in more detail the specificity of Weimar cinema.

One of the most persistent, if discredited, methods of the sociology of literature or the cinema is to posit some link between the social origins of artists and the ideological concerns of their works. With respect to German Expressionism this has been done most extensively by George Huaco, who attempts to account for the 'conservative' nature of German films by pointing out that almost all directors and producers of the classic German cinema were middle-class, conservatively educated, university-trained men.[57] However, it seems to me that social origins are probably less important than the tendencies I have outlined above. That is, given the high level of debate and self-consciousness in Germany about the 'nature' of cinema and given the embattled position *vis-à-vis* their own cultural peer-group on the one hand and the Hollywood mass market on the other, German filmmakers were nevertheless in some sense privileged. Under the guidance of producers such as Davidson and Pommer, for instance, they were positively encouraged to 'experiment' and to explore the particular effects of the apparatus. This would mean that the level at which 'society' entered into the films was not that of the sociological background and ideological beliefs of individual filmmakers, nor that of a 'reflection' of a national character, but was in the context of an ideological debate through which different groups of cultural producers vied with one another for important political terrain.

This debate was in fact about the nature of technology and the arts. In early 20th-century Germany, art and culture were in the hands of writers and artists whose convictions were firmly anti-technological. At the same time, almost all the social and economic dynamism of Germany came from its scientists, engineers and technocrats. When the *Kinodebatte* broke, it pitted spokesmen from the traditional arts, theater, books and publishing against the new form of entertainment, which seemed threatening precisely because technologically-reproduced art tended to undermine the very bases of bourgeois style: uniqueness, authenticity, personality and what Benjamin called 'aura.'[58]

The traditional emphasis on the themes of the 'fantastic,' on doubles, on the demonic, on golems and Faustian over-reachers, on mad inventors and cruel tyrant figures, on Mabuses and hypnotized, spellbound marionettes, on Caligaris and Cesares, on Nosferatus and hands of Orlac, point to the persistent fictionalization of this imaginary. These motifs, borrowed from Romanticism and the Gothic tradition, were transformed into the specific mythology of the cinema to become the very mark of a self-reflexive dialectic. This dialectic was based on the anti-technological conservative ideology of late Romanticism (where a new psychology of the unconscious elaborated its literary and fictional embodiments as it tried to formulate a response to the brutality and terror of industrialization), which collided with and at the same time articulated the film 'creator's' own participation in this technology, whose power of social control and behavioral change was beginning to become evident. In this regard, Burch is suggestive, especially in his remarks about those inventors of the cinema whose *ideé fixe* was the recreation of life in its entirety by means of a mechanical apparatus. In Burch's description of Edison and his spiritual followers we recognize not only Bazin's 'Myth of Total Cinema,'[59] but also, as Burch himself points out, a Faustian and Promethean dimension. Behind the Edisonian project of the Kinetophono-graph, he detects, rightly I think, the ambition of Frankenstein: to reproduce life artificially and mechanically, *à rebours*, so to speak, and in defiance of nature.

The German cinema of the 1920s seems to me to partake massively of the 'Edisonian' imaginary, something of which there is virtually no indication in available accounts. This cinema has, finally, little to do with the 'myth of total cinema' as a teleological fantasy of realism or with the technological goal of synchronizing vision and sound (a 'vulgar materialist' version of this imaginary). Instead, the 'defective' narratives of the Weimar cinema, their undecidability, their peculiar articulation of time and space, and their resulting problematic relation to visual pleasure and the look, all point to a form of perception that is neither altogether voyeuristic-fetishistic nor an imitation of 'normal vision' (the camera at eye-level, or the kind of rhetoric of camera-vision which Bazin designated as realistic in the work of Renoir or Rossellini).

What has entered into the textbooks is that the German cinema pioneered the extensive use of studio work, pre-production design, purpose-built sets—all of which ensured (directorial) control over lighting, camera angles and the relation of background to foreground. The result was the famous '*Stimmung*,' the unified atmosphere and look of a film. When historians have tried to account for this studio-bound conception of filmmaking, they have either posited the existence of a 'style,' such as Expressionism, or they have fallen back on anecdotal explanations, such as Lotte Eisner's (quoted earlier) about Max Reinhardt having to use *ersatz* materials which made him invent symbolic and dramatic lighting. Others have adduced the unpredictability of weather conditions as the reason why German filmmakers stayed indoors. Both sorts of explanations remain unconvincing, not because of the difficulties of establishing valid historical parallels or finding empirical evidence, but because they implicitly frame the problem as one to which such facts and data could provide meaningful answers.

If a materialist history is what is needed, a much more radical de-centering of the object of study would seem to be required. I have tried to suggest several possible vantage points from which the field would rearrange itself. Whether it is the historical or the inscribed spectator, the sexually or class-differentiated subject, or the materialization and *mise-en-scène* of a particular form of perception and vision, in each case one is faced with relations of power, control and pleasure which reach beyond film history, and even the histories of its technological and economic practices. In the case of Germany, the cinema established itself in a society transforming itself from an agrarian to an industrial country more abruptly than others, and undergoing rapid changes in its demographic and family structures. The materialist basis of Weimar cinema would in this analysis be less the overall political development of Germany on the brink of fascism, and more its part in another historical process—to which fascism is quite clearly a response—namely that which transformed, among other things, manufacture into administratively organized industrial production, and which engendered quite different demands on the human senses, faculties and skills, adding greatly to the overdevelopment of the eye.

Viewed from my own perspective, however, what is historically specific is the situation of the filmmakers rather than the audience. This encompasses their relationship not only to 'culture' and the intellectual establishment, but also to the technology and economics of the cinema. In a context where for most of them the cinema represented a break with a previous self-image or profession, and under conditions where, not unlike avant-garde movements in other countries, their work was to some extent exempt from the full pressures of the market, they nevertheless could not achieve complete socioeconomic independence insofar as they were working for commercial companies.

The typically German emphasis on effects created 'in the camera' (so admired by other directors such as Hitchcock) foregrounds the cinematic apparatus to the extent of unifying representation in subordination to the exigencies and potential of the camera and the editing table. One can understand the concept of *mise-en-scène*, as it is credited to German filmmakers, as a specifically filmic organization of views, events and their sequence whose rationale does not derive from some concrete idea of action or causal chain; instead, that organization is remotivated in particularly complex and interesting ways. The celebrated 'subjectivity' of Carl Mayer, Murnau and Karl Freund in their use of the 'unchained camera' is both an effect of how space is organized on and off screen in relation to movement, and an attempt to 'narrativize' and anthropomorphize the possibilities inherent in the camera's non-human vision. Thus it is the self-representation of the cinematic apparatus that plays the important role insofar as it can transform reality or explicitly simulate realities rather than reproduce them—including 'subjective' reality.

Although it did not conceive of itself as opposed to narrative cinema, the German cinema developed an 'experimental' side which grew directly out of the desire to conceptualize the problems of the cinema *vis-à-vis* the visible world and the subject-effects that this entailed. Murnau's fades on white or Lang's editing seem indeed to have more in common with Michael Snow or Peter Kubelka than with Griffith's use of editing and fades, in, say, *Birth of a Nation*. Whether this makes their work avant-garde is in some sense an academic question, since the cinematic avant-garde constituted itself as avant-garde under historical conditions quite different from those of Murnau, Pabst or Lang. On the other hand, this is no value judgment of D.W. Griffith. American filmmakers, and Griffith in particular, were fully exposed to commercial considerations and profit maximization as early as 1914, which is why it is reasonable to seek out economic determinants of film form.[60] But in Germany a similar *a priori* assumption would be, for the reasons suggested, more problematic.

No doubt it does make sense to be pragmatic about the different perspectives and emphases I have outlined, to add them one to the other in the hope of a synthesis whose theoretical name is 'overdetermination.' Indeed, there is a temptation to conceptualize a particular area of overlap among these various discourses: the fictions of the Weimar cinema, one might say, focus so much on power and control because they put into play the fascination with total control continually evoked by the editing and a camera-centered filmmaking. At the same time, the spectator—placed between the look of the characters and that of the camera—participates in a pleasure/power/anxiety nexus whose definition and determinations strongly suggest a psychoanalytic reading.

However, might not a model based on the notion of overdetermination open up the same vicious circle to which the search for determinants seems to lead, whereby one determining instance constantly displaces another? The positing of an 'Edisonian' imaginary (stripped of Burch's binarism and immersed in another kind of dialectic—that of the camera's and the spectator's looks) is meant to suggest not a new ultimate cause vying with all the others, but a repositioning of the terms. The moment one gives priority to an emphasis on *Schaulust*, on fascination with specific cinema-effects, or (in the case of the German cinema) on *mise-en-scène*, it can be seen that the history of the cinema—conceived as a search for determinants—cannot be presented as an addition of constituent parts or partial histories in the manner envisaged by Nowell-Smith.

The emphasis on *mise-en-scène* in relation to visual pleasure stresses that the cinema is an apparatus for the articulation of an imaginary (sense of) time and space. What seems to recommend Weimar cinema for consideration as an avant-garde practice are its formal particularities: its different treatment of time and space, its non-linear, non-causal conceptions of sequence and narrative in the context of a fictional , imaginary dimension. It shares these properties with other social machines of *mise-en-scène* and the imaginary, such as architecture, the totalitarian state, transport systems, communication networks, the legal system and administration. In this respect, the German cinema never modelled itself on the large social machines of production, as did the Soviet cinema in the 1920s. What makes Weimar cinema historical—in the sense of transitional as well as of consequence—is the prominence it gives to this *mise-en-scène* of the (cinematic) imaginary.

That this imaginary is typically German would be an absurd assertion. That it is typically male would be worth arguing at greater length. It could certainly be demonstrated that its notion of visual control and transparency aims at a form of creativity which seeks to 'rearticulate' the female entirely within its own system of duplication, doubling, mirroring and transcription.[61] But additionally, this imaginary of the *mise-en-scène* strikes at the very heart of causation, difference, nature or history: all it knows are effects and the pleasures or anxieties of a world free of determinants. What is remarkable about the films of Weimar Germany is that here was a bourgeois cinema which for a given time could conceptualize the relations between different machines of *mise-en-scène*, and it did so by suspending the time-space continuum, the causality that was 'history' for the 19th century. Classical narrative, on the other hand, recreates and remotivates this time-space continuum and gives a new lease on life to the notion of history, so that even the histories of cinema tend to be formed on the basis of models of unilinear determination or classical narratives.

The Weimar cinema has never been a particularly popular cinema. It has always been something of a filmmakers' or film scholars' cinema. This makes its historical status all the more difficult to grasp. The specific features of German cinema cannot be understood in terms of some essence, some typical national character or a particular obsession, but as the moment where in retrospect something became apparent. Perhaps the properly ideological role of the cinema and its sweeping popularity only began when this particular imaginary was elided in favor of family melodrama and family romance, when the oscillation and the hesitation ceased and classical narrative became the veritable imaginary of both history and the subject. Psychoanalysis, as the most coherent theory of the subject, may well be the last history of the cinema, because unlike competing paradigms, it has no need for a teleology or a mythology of origins. The confrontation of psychoanalysis and cinema clearly does not have explanation or a causal model as its goal, but instead elaborates a tautology, a series of duplication effects, which may be precisely what is at stake. In other words, the history of the cinema may well be the analysis of its reduplications and repetitions. Today, for example, the emphasis placed on special effects and a very evident fetishism of the apparatus in film, television and video games indicates that the relation between technology and narrative may be undergoing another shift. The Edisonian imaginary appears to return, this time not as the imaginary of the filmmaker but as that of the spectator. If so, the history of visual pleasure is in the process of beginning another chapter.

NOTES

1. Michel Foucault, *Archeology of Knowledge*, trans. A.M. Sheridan-Smith (New York: Pantheon Books, 1972), p. 230.

2. Robert C. Allen, 'Film History: The Narrow Discourse,' in *Film: Historical-Theoretical Explorations*, ed. Ben Lawton and Janet Staiger (Pleasantville, NY: Redgrave Publishing, 1977), pp. 9-10.

3. Will Straw, 'The Myth of Total Cinema History,' *Ciné-Tracts*, vol. 3, no. 1 (1980), p. 8.

4. Edward Buscombe, 'A New Approach to Film History,' in *Film: Historical-Theoretical Explorations*, p. 1.

5. Charles F. Altman, 'Towards a Historiography of American Film,' *Cinema Journal*, vol. 16, no. 2 (1977), pp. 1-2.

6. Douglas Gomery, 'Mode of Production, Hollywood, and Finance Capitalism: A Reformulation' (unpublished paper presented at the 1979 Milwaukee Film Theory Conference), p. 2.

7. John Ellis, 'The Institution of Cinema,' *Edinburgh Magazine*, no. 2 (1977), p. 57.

8. Geoffrey Nowell-Smith, 'On the Writing of the History of the Cinema: Some Problems,' *Edinburgh Magazine*, no. 2 (1977), p. 12.

9. Harry Reasoner, on *60 Minutes* (CBS, June 1982).

10. Ellis, p. 63.

11. See, for instance, Constance Penley, 'The Avant-Garde and its Imaginary,' *Camera Obscura*, no. 2 (1977).

12. Christian Metz, *Le Signifiant imaginaire* (Paris: Union Générale d'Editions, 1977).

13. For some general thoughts on this topic, see my 1969 article 'Narrative Cinema and Audience-Oriented Aesthetics,' in *Popular Television and Film*, ed. T. Bennet *et al.* (London: BFI/Open University, 1982), and my 'Screen Violence and *A Clockwork Orange*,' in *Approaches to Popular Culture*, ed. C. Bigsby (London: Edward Arnold, 1976).

14. Lotte Eisner, *The Haunted Screen* (Los Angeles, CA: University of California Press, 1969); Siegfried Kracauer, *From Caligari to Hitler* (Princeton, NJ: Princeton University Press, 1947); George Huaco, *Sociology of Film* (New York: Basic Books, 1965); Andrew Tudor, *Image and Influence* (New York: St. Martin's Press, 1974); Paul Monaco, *Cinema and Society: Germany and France during the Twenties* (New York: Elsevier/Nelson Books, 1976).

15. Nowell-Smith, p. 11.

16. In a recent German edition, the editor, Karsten Witte, is at pains to point out how misleading the English 'to Hitler' of the title can be: instead of translating it '*bis Hitler*' (i.e., terminal), he translates it '*zu Hitler*' (in the direction of). Siegfried Kracauer, *Von Caligari zu*

Hitler (Frankfurt: Suhrkamp, 1981). The edition also contains all of Kracauer's original film reviews.

17. Noël Burch, 'Porter or Ambivalence,' trans. Tom Milne, *Screen*, vol. 19, no. 4 (1978-1979), p. 103.

18. Pascal Bonitzer, 'It's Only a Film,' trans. Martyn Auty, *Framework*, no. 14 (1981), p. 23.

19. See Mary Ann Doane, '*The Student of Prague*' (unpublished paper, University of Iowa, 1978).

20. Burch, p. 99.

21. Noël Burch and Jorge Dana, 'Propositions,' trans. Diana Matias and Christopher King, *Afterimage*, no. 5 (1974).

22. See Kracauer, *Von Caligari zu Hitler*, for valuable information on Kracauer's intellectual position *vis-à-vis* the Marxism of the Frankfurt School and the *Neue Sachlichkeit*.

23. For a more detailed analysis of a Weimar 'oedipal narrative,' see my article on Pabst's *Pandora's Box* (*Screen*, vol. 24, nos. 4-5 [1983]).

24. Pamela Falkenberg, 'Oedipal Structures in French and German Films' (unpublished paper, University of Iowa, 1978).

25. Kracauer, *From Caligari to Hitler*, p. 6.

26. Mary Ann Doane, 'Narrative Strategies in Weimar Cinema' (unpublished paper, University of Iowa, 1978).

27. Samuel Weber, 'The Sideshow: or Remarks on a Canny Moment,' *MLN*, vol. 88, no. 6 (1973), p. 1133.

28. Doane, 'Narrative Strategies.'

29. See, for instance, Wilhelm Reich, *The Mass Psychology of Fascism*, trans. Vincent R. Carfagno (New York: Farrar, Straus & Giroux, 1980).

30. Doane, 'Narrative Strategies.'

31. Patricia Mellencamp, 'Oedipus and the Robot in *Metropolis*,' *Enclitic*, vol. 5, no. 1 (1981), p. 25.

32. 'I feel . . . my exclusion from desire, while reminding myself that "logic" is also an historical discourse.' Ibid., p. 40.

33. See Klaus Theweleit, *Männerphantasien* (Reinbek: Rowohlt, 1980).

34. Kracauer, *From Caligari to Hitler*, p. 11.

35. See my 'Social Mobility and the Fantastic in Weimar Films,' *Wide Angle*, vol. 5, no. 2 (1982).

36. Richard de Cordova, 'The Weimar Frame Tale' (unpublished paper, University of Iowa, 1978).

37. Siegfried Kracauer, *Das Ornament der Masse* (Frankfurt: Suhrkamp, 1963), p. 279, my translation.

38. Kracauer, *From Caligari to Hitler*, p. v.

39. Kracauer, *Das Ornament der Masse*, p. 280.

40. See, for instance, Leo Handel, *Hollywood Looks at Its Audiences* (Urbana, IL: University of Illinois Press, 1950).

41. Kracauer, *From Caligari to Hitler*, p. 11.

42. See my 'Myth as the Phantasmagoria of History,' *New German Critique*, nos. 24-25 (1981-1982).

43. For an interestingly different analysis, see Michel Henry, *Le Cinéma expressioniste allemand* (Montpellier: Editions du Signe, 1971).

44. See my 'Primary Identification and the Historical Subject,' *Ciné-Tracts*, vol. 3, no. 3 (1980).

45. Tony Kaes, ed., *Kinodebatte* (Munich: Deutscher Taschenbuch Verlag; and Tübingen: Max Niemeyer, 1978).

46. Erich Pommer, quoted in Huaco, gives a succinct account of some of the motives involved in making *The Cabinet of Dr. Caligari*.

47. This policy was vindicated by 'history' insofar as it is precisely the films of the German art cinema that have survived.

48. 'During the later years of the First War, Max Reinhardt . . . was obliged by shortage of raw materials . . . to discontinue the grandeur of his productions. . . . Light and darkness then took on a new meaning, by replacing structural variety and by animating and transforming a single set; shifting lighting-effects, crossing and clashing with one another, were the only means of disguising the mediocrity of the ersatz materials . . . and of varying the intensity of the atmosphere to suit the action.' (Eisner, p. 48.)

49. George Mosse, *The Nationalization of the Masses* (New York: Howard Fertig, 1975), p. 207.

50. Karsten Witte, 'Visual Pleasure Inhibited,' *New German Critique*, nos. 24–25 (1981–1982), p. 239 (translation modified).

51. Georg Lukács, *History and Class Consciousness*, trans. Rodney Livingstone (Cambridge, MA: MIT Press, 1971).

52. Walter Benjamin, 'On Some Motifs in Baudelaire,' in *Illuminations*, trans. Harry Zohn (New York: Schocken Books, 1969), p. 163.

53. See, for instance, Norbert Elias, *The Civilizing Process*, trans. Edmund Jephcott (New York: Urizen Books, 1978).

54. See, for another view of this, my '*Lili Marleen*: Fascism and the Film Industry,' *October*, no. 21 (1982).

55. Noël Burch, *To the Distant Observer* (London: Scolar Press, 1979), pp. 61-66.

56. For a very interesting discussion of cinematic *bricolage*, see Michael Chanan, *The Dream That Kicked* (London: Routledge & Kegan Paul, 1980).

57. Huaco, p. 87.

58. For a discussion of Weimar 'Mandarin culture' in relation to the cinema, see John Tulloch, 'Genetic Structuralism,' *Australian Journal of Screen Theory*, no. 1 (1977).

59. André Bazin, 'The Myth of Total Cinema,' in *What is Cinema?*, vol. I, trans. Hugh Gray (Los Angeles, CA: University of California Press, 1967).

60. See Tom Gunning, 'Weaving a Narrative,' *Quarterly Review of Film Studies*, vol. 6, no. 1 (1981).

61. For a classic statement of the Edisonian imaginary as a male fantasy, see Villiers de l'Isle-Adam, *L'Eve future* (1886; rpt. Paris: J.J. Pauvert, 1960).

II

CINEMA PRACTICES

What Is a Camera?

Edward Branigan

What is a camera? At first glance, the answer seems obvious. We know perfectly well what a camera is. But then again, perhaps the very confidence with which we answer should cause us to hesitate. One of the lessons Noam Chomsky teaches (with respect to the concept 'grammatical') is that some of the most important things to analyze and to explicate are precisely our intuitions—those beliefs which appear self-evident and certain.

The question: What is a camera? bears a resemblance to André Bazin's famous question: What is cinema?[1] as well as to an even larger investigation: What is art? These questions, phrased in this way, seem to call for a special kind of definition that points out a shared essence, an inherent quality, which marks the particular object—camera, cinema, art—and simultaneously distinguishes it from all other objects for all time; for example, the uniqueness of an object's existence might be defined as a set of necessary and sufficient conditions. Problems have arisen, however, in asking this sort of general question and so our first task should be to reformulate the question by avoiding the ontological verb form, 'is.' (The word 'is' derives, of course, from the infinitive 'to be,' whose gerund form, 'being,' suggests an inquiry into the fundamental and irreducible nature of something.) I propose instead to ask, how does the word 'camera' function in the language we use to talk about cinema?[2] What does 'camera' mean as a critical term? How is it meaningful to us within the cinematic institution?

The introduction of such words as 'function' and 'meaning' suggests that the notion of camera must be located within a more general inquiry into the nature of signification. What do we mean by 'meaning'?[3] For present purposes, I will assume that a theory of meaning, in its most general form, seeks to elaborate the relationship between an entity *present* to our senses and another entity *absent* to our senses; that is, when we experience one thing, something *else* might also come to mind. The present entity may be, for example, a shape drawn in ink or registered through the chemicals of a film emulsion while the absent entity may be an 'idea,' a 'feeling,' a 'memory,' or an object elsewhere in the world. How is it, then, that a present entity, A, *stands for* (or stands in for) something else, B, which is absent? The answer as to what constitutes 'presence' and 'absence' and how these are related to a perceiver can be located only within a particular theory of meaning. Not surprisingly, many processes have been advanced as an explanation of the overall movement from presence to absence, and additional distinctions have been made concerning preliminary, intermediate and subsequent stages.

It is my belief that the notion of camera is inextricably bound up with the above sorts of questions about meaning, that a critic's statement about camerawork is ultimately a claim about how film is able to generate meaning and emotion in a spectator. This suggests that quite a number of cameras are possible in accord with various theories of meaning, and that one critic's camera is not necessarily that of another critic. In order to examine these different usages, I will limit myself to narrative film. This means that the sort of camera a critic postulates will also depend upon the *value* assigned to narrative by his or her society; that is, narrativity is not something private and individual but arises in a historical setting and serves particular needs of a community. The type of *history* we write about narrative, in turn, will be a summation of our beliefs as to what counts as narrative, what it is used for, and what it ought to be. More generally, our notion of the camera is, in the end, governed both by our assumptions about the process of meaning in narrative and by the value of narrative to society; or rather, we might say that our theory of meaning itself has a social value and responds to our deepest beliefs about society.

I now wish to survey eight major conceptions of the camera in order to demonstrate their connections to various narrative theories and social values. If this enables us to rethink the concept of camera—or at least to gain some distance from it—then the way is open to reformulate our conception of narrative and the way we write the history of narrative. I want to emphasize at the outset that I will not be arguing for a grand, new camera as the sum of all the old ones, for that would be a peculiarly unwieldly one and would merely recapitulate the histories already written about narrative cinema. My goal is simply to unwind the beliefs to which we are committed when we employ the word 'camera' in a particular way. I will conclude by suggesting what areas of research have been opened by the most recent theories of the camera.

It will be helpful to begin by examining the camera's role in producing the initial visual stimulus which is seen by the viewer. When we use the word camera to describe the organization of immediate sensory data, to what are we referring? The clearest and most convincing example of this role of the camera is the kinetic depth effect. (See the accompanying diagram.)[4] One can devise an experiment in which the shadow of an object is thrown onto a screen to be viewed by a spectator. The shadow, of course, is two-dimensional. However, if the object is rotated by a motor, the spectator will immediately see a three-dimensional shape on the screen even though the moving shadows remain two-dimensional. The reason is that the human perceptual system is able to utilize the *motion* of the shadows to *construct* a three-dimensional entity which is not directly visible. Applying this experiment to cinema, we can say that the motor which rotates the object is analogous to the motion picture camera which gently turns the world for our inspection. Here the camera, like the motor, becomes the unifying principle of a sensory display. The camera becomes the simplest hypothesis[5] or (unconscious)

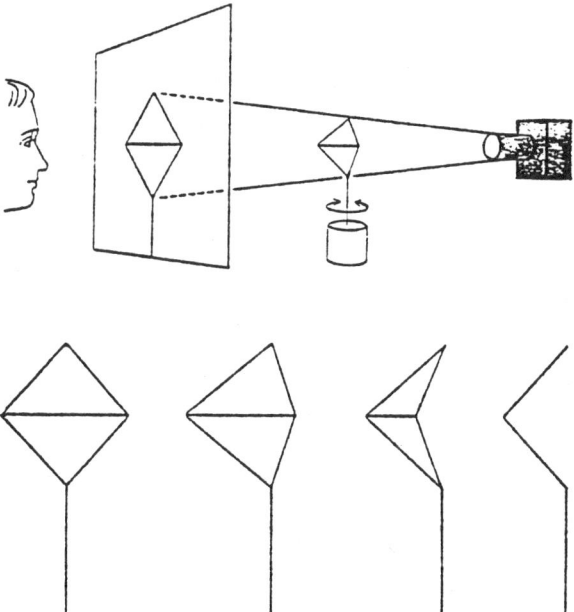

KINETIC DEPTH EFFECT shows how movement can endow perceived objects with three-dimensional shape. The shadow of a bent wire form (shown at bottom in four different orientations) looks as flat as the screen on which it is cast so long as the form remains stationary. When it is swiveled back and forth, the changing shadow is seen as a rigid rotating object with the appropriate three-dimensionality. The direction of rotation remains ambiguous.

Illustration and text from Ulric Neisser, 'The Processes of Vision.' Copyright © 1968 by *Scientific American, Inc.* All rights reserved.

deduction that we can make about a changing set of stimuli: through its agency, shadows are transformed into three-dimensional objects.

In this approach, meaning is a percept which can be studied through the methods and theories of sensory psychology. The camera becomes one aspect of a complex perceptual process linking something present on a screen to something absent or beyond the screen. These perceptual processes form the basis of an *illusion* theory of meaning.[6] Plato's famous application of the concept of illusion to art is explicitly recalled in such modern theories as those of E.H. Gombrich and, for film, Jean-Louis Baudry.[7] Noël Burch spells out the consequences for the camera in such a theory by arguing that certain camera techniques can break the spell of illusion which normally binds a spectator to the film; for example, he argues for 'surface' over 'depth' effects and for 'gratuitous' camera movements.[8] Histories of narrative can then be constructed which trace the degrees to which cinema succumbs to or escapes from perceptual illusion. Thus one might oppose the filmmakers who supposedly promoted illusion—Edison, Porter, Dickson, Raff and Gammon, Smith, Ince, Griffith, De Mille—to those who viewed cinema as toy or as science—Méliès, Lumière, Marey, Muybridge, Warhol, Godard, Snow, O'Neill.[9]

It is not enough, however, in writing a history of narrative forms, to understand the details of various illusion theories. One also needs to understand why the theories were popular; that is, how does the concept of illusion operate within a given historical setting to articulate the needs and issues of that community? For instance, the Church in Renaissance Italy decided that the positive values of a heightened illusion of reality in paintings based on Biblical narratives (fostered principally by the development of linear perspective) outweighed—but just barely—its dangers (idolatry).[10] One might also argue that illusionism expressed the interests of a rising merchant class and that realistic depictions aimed at a different economic strata must take another form. The point here is that a term like 'camera' assumes its place within a larger theory of narrative production (in this case, as building on illusion) as well as within, or against, the values assigned to that production by a particular society.

So far we have considered the camera as the origin of an illusory sensation (e.g., of depth), but a second approach would hold that it is simply sensation—a sensory *form* to be experienced in its own right. This approach, typified by Noël Burch's early work, takes as its starting point a complete inventory of the possible forms and types of sensation.[11] The camera becomes one of many parameters to be manipulated and varied across the film as a whole. The goal is to select forms which will force themselves on a spectator's attention by breaking with his or her habitual and practical, everyday experience. Thus the spectator becomes the site for shock effects: discontinuity, provocation, disorientation. The key criterion for the camera is a demand to make the world unfamiliar, strange, new. Forms present to our senses on, for example, a theater screen bring absent entities to our attention through a process of 'defamiliarization.'[12]

What is unfamiliar depends on what is familiar which, in turn, depends on the dominant forms of realism in a particular historical setting. Hence this conception of the camera is always defined against a historical standard and shifts with the times to maintain its adversary position. The result often is that the history of film is conceived in terms of an avant-garde whose mission is to refuse the dominant practice and explore frontiers.[13] The camera ideally becomes active, even obtrusive; in Eisenstein's phrase, 'hewing out a piece of actuality with the ax of the lens.'[14]

When we abandon the notion of the camera as an adversary to the world, however, and instead emphasize its 'natural' connections to the world, we reach another, more orthodox version of the camera. This approach stresses the necessary, scientific link among objects, light rays, and film emulsion. Across this (one-way) bridge, reality passes into the film and its representations. The camera escapes being mere sensation and becomes a token of the world. What is present on the screen is causally related, in the manner of a fingerprint, asserts Bazin, to absent entities.[15] Not only objects can be recorded in this manner but, as Arthur Danto notes, the camera itself, especially through its movement, makes the 'mode of recording part of the record';[16] that is, the camera, too, leaves a photographic mark frozen in time. Nevertheless, the resulting conception of the camera is decidedly static. The camera is reduced to an act of ostension, a gesture pointing toward objects and occasionally toward itself as object: 'Look *here* at *this*.' Thus some writers have held that photography is simply too real, and allows the photographer too little creative control, to be a genuine art form.[17] In that case, as Roger Scruton believes:

> The history of the art of photography is the history of successive attempts to break the causal chain by which the photographer is imprisoned, to impose a human intention between [an object] and [its] appearance so that the [object] can be both defined by that intention and seen [by us] in terms of it.[18]

The remarkable subtlety of Bazin's theory is due in large measure to a powerful synthesis of two conceptions of the camera. The first—just mentioned—compels the camera through physical law to record a *profilmic* reality. At the same time, however, a second force binds the camera to a *postfilmic* reality. This second component of the camera is the reality of a spectator's viewing situation, and it is controlled by perceptual law. Realism in the cinema, according to Bazin, is not merely due to the scientific basis of the photographic image but also, he insists, is based on 'those conditions which respect certain physiological or mental facts of natural perception or, more exactly, in rediscovering *equivalents* for them.'[19] Bazin asserts that a 'universal psychological experience' underlies the many devices of film. He declares that 'Our legs and neck didn't wait for the cinema to invent the tracking shot and the pan, nor our attention to contrive the close-up.'[20] Note that the effect of this type of comparison is twofold: the turn of a spectator's head acquires a mechanical component (which may be duplicated) while, at the same time, the camera becomes more human.

Bazin is not alone in searching for filmic equivalents to human perception. Karel Reisz, Gavin Millar, and Ernest Lindgren likewise employ psychological premises, although they reach different conclusions. In fact, these writers effectively reverse Bazin's prejudice in favor of the long take, and instead posit editing as the essence of cinema.[21] Camera movement for them becomes simply another method of transferring the spectator's attention (analogous to eye movement, according to Lindgren)[22] and is therefore treated as a subcategory of editing.[23] In the present context, I am less interested in the particular conclusions drawn from various psychological premises than in the logic employed: in each instance a specific film technique is traced back to a putative 'normal mental mechanism by which we alter our attention from object to object in real life.'[24] For Reisz, Millar and Lindgren editing is fundamental; for Bazin, the image and the camera. The methods of reasoning, however, are identical.

For Bazin, the camera, acted upon by reality, must react in place of an absent spectator, but only in ways which are homologous with the laws of human perception. Two of the cinematic techniques championed by Bazin are deep focus in on-screen space and 'lateral depth of field'[25] in the activation of off-screen space. The two techniques complement one another and serve to unite the two main strands in Bazin's work dealing with profilmic and postfilmic realities beyond the image. Deep focus, for him, means 'non-selective' focus, hence a gain in the perceiver's ability to select freely what is important. At the same time, certain kinds of lateral camera movements also increase the perceiver's confidence in his or her own independence: the freedom not only to scan an image but to predict what will or *could* be shown at its edges at any moment.[26] The overall aim is to ensure that the perceiver sees present entities on the screen in the exact way he or she *would see* absent entities, including absent entities which are off-screen and perhaps *never* shown![27] In such a theory, the value of narrativity for society lies in releasing documentary reality and disclosing real conditions of vision and viewing.[28] 'Comments' by an author or manipulations of plot may obscure but cannot finally defeat such Bazinian properties of the world as ambiguity, multiplicity, chance, independence, continuity, density, detail and even mystery. For Bazin, a neorealist documentary lies hidden within every narrative.

Realism, then, for Bazin is a complex interaction between conditions forced on the camera by the profilmic and the postfilmic. It is opposed by narrative and 'expressionism' which comprise all those tricks of the trade—the artifice—that a filmmaker can summon to stimulate and guide a spectator's attention—principally through plot and montage. Realism versus expressionism, however, quickly becomes a brutal duality perpetuated in many histories of film narrative by opposing the work of Louis Lumière and Georges Méliès. In addition, this duality is reflected in the most common and durable refrain in all of orthodox criticism, whether applied to film or any of the other arts; namely, the spectator must never become aware of the actual techniques employed by the artwork, for that reveals not reality and truth but the contrivance of an individual—the artist. Camerawork must never be 'obvious' or become 'obtrusive.'[29]

Narrative, too, is subject to this 'unobtrusiveness' principle. The history of narrative is interpreted as an evolution in search of a satisfying accomodation between the extremes of realism and expressionism—of vulgar naturalism and crude artifice.[30] It should be said that although Bazin remains within this orthodox tradition, he emphasizes not so much an 'evolution' as a 'dialectical' interaction between the extremes.[31] He maintains that the favored techniques (e.g., deep focus) are neither necessary nor sufficient to reveal reality; one also needs the insight and contrivances of the artist.[32]

We have reached a point now where a central issue in defining the camera is the postfilmic viewing situation. If we therefore broaden our investigation to include the general psychology of the viewer, we arrive at another conception of the camera. This camera is meant to serve and reveal human consciousness in its full range of feelings and motives, not just its ways of perceiving. The process is termed *expression*, a word which derives from Latin and means literally 'to press out,' that is, to force outward that which is hidden within. What is present on the screen for our inspection is the residue of some other person's private state of consciousness. For example, the so-called subjective camera can be used to depict a character who is seated, walking, drunk, dizzy, fearful, dreaming, remembering, and so forth. Other, more 'neutral' shots are still based on this model; it is simply more difficult to ascertain whose consciousness is being portrayed. The so-called 'perfect view' shot,[33] for example, represents the attention of an invisible, ideal observer.[34] Ultimately, our task as spectators in an expressionist theory is to reconstruct through empathy the vision and emotions not only of characters, observers and narrators but also of the author—the original and First Cause. In this sense, empathy functions merely as the inverse of intention. We are to look within ourselves to understand the feelings being portrayed—pressed out—through the intentional act of an author. Empathy and intention complement one another because they draw on a presumed universal psychology of human beings. Thus, what began as the simple inspection of an externalized state of another concludes with a decisive look inward accompanied by heightened feelings of recognition and revelation.

Expression theories grew from the Romantic movement of the first half of the 19th century and stressed the creative sensibilities of a lone individual.[35] The artwork is said to achieve congruence with an internal state by means of simple reflection,[36] the operation of innate brain fields,[37] or sheer willpower—the intention of an author who forces us to recognize ourselves. According to the last, the director of a film wields the camera as a pen or a paintbrush for our benefit.[38] A history of narrative film written on this basis becomes essentially a random collection of anecdotes about individuals who, touched by genius, have triumphed over all obstacles and become great teachers. The resulting film history is little more than Andrew Sarris' 'Directorial Chronology 1915-1967.'[39]

A new sort of camera emerges, however, to the extent that the spectator is assigned a somewhat more central role in the production of meaning. If we interpret the expression of the author as something other than a self-serving display of consciousness to be absorbed and imitated by a spectator, and instead emphasize the fact of a purposeful *communication*, we arrive at the idea that an apparent transmission of information has occurred for the benefit of someone. In a communication theory of narrative, the narration assumes a literal sense: a translation of *knowing* into *telling* followed by a reconversion by the spectator of telling into knowing.[40] The attitude or viewpoint of an author, or at least some species of narrator, is transmitted with minimal resistance (lessened by the critic) to the spectator. The outcome is knowledge about reality, inflected by the narrator's view of it. The nature of the causal connection between sender and receiver—which is rooted in the mathematics of information theory—must be carefully adjusted as a communication model is applied to language in general, to literature, and to film.[41]

The function of the camera in such a scheme is, I believe, analogous to what Roman Jakobson describes as the *phatic* element in language.[42] The camera (along with other aspects of the film) provides the physical and psychological *channel* by which we enter and remain in communication. One could perhaps go further and define certain camera maneuvers analogous to the ritualized formulas of the phatic which seek to establish, prolong, scrutinize and break off communication. ('Shall we start? Do you see? Watch this! Are you still interested?') In general, the camera allows us, as well as a variety of implied observers and narratees within the text, to remain in (imperfect) contact with a variety of implied authors, narrators and characters, all willing to speak and show things to us. Our primary task is to discover with whom we are in contact: to discover, in Nick Browne's words, the 'narrating agency or authority which can be taken to rationalize the presentation of shots' and in addition, one assumes, the presentation of shot transitions, camera movements, sounds, etc.[43] Critics have described an amazing array of narrators in films, including the 'collective' consciousness of a village and of Paris; the 'central' consciousness of various characters, of a donkey, of God, and even of inanimate objects.[44] It is no wonder, then, that the camera itself can be awakened to consciousness and so described in blatantly anthropomorphic terms. A pan is again like the turn of someone's head but no longer that of a character or of the Bazinian spectator. The camera acquires a will of its own. Accordingly, it has been described by critics as bold, curious, lewd, tactful, exhibiting a sense of smell, and 'smiling ironically.'[45] One assumes, as well, that it has an ear for conversation. Whatever stands out as 'unrealistic' or 'intrusive' in a film can be conveniently reinterpreted as the camera's or the narrator's 'commentary' (i.e., a message). The 'unobtrusiveness principle,' characteristic of profilmic theories of the camera, is here effectively reversed so that it is now laudable when a film flaunts its artifice and becomes self-conscious and reflexive. At this point communication begins to slide back toward an expressive theory and the reconstruction of intentional and empathic states.

Communication theories, with their emphasis on rhetoric and commentary, are particularly adept at dealing with 'difficult' films like those of the art cinema. A history of narrative can be based upon the increasing exploitation and awareness of authorial forms of address: overt commentary, irony, ambiguity, metaphor, playfulness, enigmatic presentations, etc.[46] Unusual camera movements become the very mark of narration; the insistence on framing becomes a compulsion to tell, which surpasses a merely photographic simulacrum of the world.

However, if we now dissect the notion of communication—both the compulsion to tell and the corresponding compulsion to watch and listen— we may find at the center of these impulses unconscious desires and wish-fulfillment rather than simple messages. This leads to a new type of camera where the notion of an exchange of messages by persons is replaced by a theory of what it means to be a person. The text becomes a *fantasy* scene, created and mutually sustained by a viewer and an author, each forming a distinct identity with/against the imagined Other. Just as the subject is split into conscious and unconscious, so the text has a manifest and a latent, or repressed, level. Meaning for a subject depends upon a movement from secondary to primary processes of the psychical apparatus: a descent from present sensation, governed by the reality principle, toward what is absent from consciousness—instinctual energy and pleasure.[47] Psychoanalysis provides the theory of this movement. Since it teaches a certain skepticism about what is immediately conscious to us, it is not surprising that many writers employing this methodology view cinema as an illusory presentation.[48] The camera functions along with conventions of editing, lighting, etc., to either foster or break our spell of belief. Earlier we examined the components of an illusionary theory of the camera.

There is another possibility for the camera, however, within the psychoanalytic approach. The camera can be conceived as part of a special process which acts to represent the fantasies of dream-thought. Unconscious impulses, no matter how abstract, must be transformed into visual images in order to appear in dream. This means that thoughts which admit of visual representation will be preferred and that others will be displaced toward pictorial substitutes.[49] The camera accomplishes these tasks in ways which often escape our notice, so that one might properly speak of two cameras within the psychoanalytic mode: one is manifest (and illusory), and the other repressed. Paul Willemen has provided some examples from the work of Max Ophuls. He demonstrates how a verbal metaphor can be transformed quite literally into a camera movement which *at the same time* reveals the repression that the original word has sought to conceal.[50]

It is apparent that the unconscious mechanisms studied by psychoanalysis outrun the usual categories applied to a history of narrative forms, such as style, genre, period, nationality, writer, director and studio. A more appropriate category would seem to be 'mode of discourse,' which is to say a broad group of texts enacting a limited matrix of preoccupations and resolutions (i.e., a class of texts in search of a particular libidinal economy). Psychoanalysis shares with illusionist theories of narrative the need for principles of grouping based upon various effects on a viewer. Thus far, study has focused principally on the so-called classical narrative. Within this discourse it has been argued that the camera repeats phallic aggression while giving visual form to the unconscious of a patriarchal society.[51]

However, one cannot dream in languages one does not already know. For this reason Christian Metz argues that an understanding of the primary process of the unconscious also requires an analysis of the secondary process. Contributing to this latter analysis are the disciplines of phenomenology, linguistics, symbolic logic and cognitive psychology.[52] The result of applying certain insights from these fields is that cinema is conceived as a language in which meaning is symbolic.[53] That is, present entities refer to absent entities through the operation of *rules* shared by a community; for example, the relation of denotation, or, for natural language, the conversion of a sentence from passive to active.

In such a scheme the camera can no longer be conceived as a real object in a profilmic or postfilmic reality which moves as humans do in order to relay the point of view either of an observer (a pan being like a turn of the head) or of no one (= the world objectified). Instead, the text is rid of misleading anthropomorphisms.[54] The 'humanism' which sustains those anthropomorphisms is relocated elsewhere within a larger, endless process of society fabricating meaning for itself according to the limits of prescribed rules (of behavior, of interpretation).[55] The claim is that it is a social system, and not an *a priori* conception of human nature, which defines what qualities will count as being 'human.' Applying this approach to textual problems, we can say that instead of seeking the residual traces of human narrators, we should concentrate on the existing rules by which a community of readers manipulates symbols and so creates the text. In the case of film, for example, Metz believes that the camera is embedded in the text as a 'purely cinematographic' signifier which is not standing in by default for an absent observer, but rather is a signifier linked through community rules to a narrative signified.[56] What interests me, however, is a slightly different formulation which begins with the spectator and then asks, how is the camera *of use* to someone in watching a film? What place does the 'camera' occupy in the account of our perception that we render, often implicitly, to ourselves? The answer, I suggest, is that the camera becomes a reading hypothesis about space—a *label* applied to the text by the viewer. This formulation attempts to capture the viewer's activity in processing a sequence of images—in fixing the position and movement of space—and to foreground the rules by which we apply labels.

The sort of camera we project in watching a film is quite unlike the actual machine employed in original photography. Consider, for example, the strange kind of camera we postulate in watching the following: animated cartoons, optical effects, swish pans, films built up from stop motion photography (i.e., pixillation effects), split screen effects (how many cameras: one, two, or three?), Michael Snow's *La Région centrale*,[57] the staircase shot in *Vertigo*,[58] and such special effects as a tracking shot through a miniature of a village in Frank Borzage's *Secrets* or past a spacecraft in *Star Wars*. In the last case we may simply see a spacecraft which moves instead of a camera which moves and we will certainly be in a different relation to the object than that of the original profilmic camera.

If we do not see through a profilmic camera, then how exactly are we seeing? I believe that the viewer is in a different place, so to speak, than the profilmic camera. The reason is that the viewer is actively constructing the space of a scene—joining fragments into a whole, recognizing implied spaces—as well as remembering the organization of past spaces and continually forming conjectures about new spaces. The so-called illusion of three-dimensional space created by the classical film is complete not when a profilmic camera has shown everything in the room—which, anyway, is usually prohibited by the 180 degree rule—but is complete when the viewer is able to imagine himself or herself in various places *apart from* the optical view. Understanding a scene entails the ability to project *new* spaces from *new* angles—whether or not we have actually seen these spaces—thus 'filling-in' gaps in the presentation of the scene. A viewer can demonstrate this ability to predict space by imagining being in the scene and moving about to assume new angles, or by drawing the scene from a new angle (e.g., an overhead view) which describes where characters and objects must be located. Such a drawing should be understood not in relation to a profilmic camera which moves about, or has moved, in a real space but as being itself fictional, as a record of the hypotheses and predictions made by a viewer about underlying connections and structure. What might be termed the 'classical camera' is simply the invitation to test a certain set of hypotheses. The viewer sees what he or she already knows, expects and desires under the generic label 'camera.' When the viewer's confidence in his or her predictions is high, the film achieves 'reality.'

Perhaps an analogy would clarify the idea of a camera which is the construction of a spectator. Rudolf Arnheim contends that one of the ways that an observer understands the composition of a painting is by hypothesizing the effects of gravity.[59] By imagining (or presuming) a downward force field acting on the graphic forms, the observer is able to bring out relevant features of the composition, e.g., symmetry, balance, pattern, 'weight' and others. (This explains why rotating an abstract painting through 90 degree angles often produces a series of startlingly distinct pictures.) My contention is that the 'camera' is a hypothesis of this sort and can be used successfully to expose pertinent features of texts.[60] Our recognition of camera movement serves to assign an orientation to space by ordering our inferences; that is, it permits us to test our beliefs about film space and time and to experience a certain measured surprise as we revise these beliefs. The word 'camera' comes to stand for a way of viewing in which we justify a (preexistent) procedure of looking. It may well be, however, that modes of discourse other than the classical text demand different sorts of reading procedures and solicit labels other than, say, establishing shot, follow shot, reaction shot, point-of-view shot, etc. This does not mean that we are all becoming more skilled and sophisticated as readers, but rather that the rules of language—the conditions of intelligibility for a community—change and that this change is correlated with a change in the social situation.

Today, the camera seems less a worldly object with a privileged access to reality and more an aspect of a collective subjectivity—merely a name for how we look and know at a particular time. As such, its status fluctuates in the twilight area between subject and object, perhaps as a symptom of our uncertainty over the very categories of subject and object. Hence, the notion of camera seems to depend finally upon how the members of a particular society *agree* to confront the material objects of existence. For this reason any project which attempts to recast the history of film narrative, and the social values narrativity serves, must at the same time rethink the concept of camera and how we have used that word.

TABLE

A COMPARISON OF EIGHT CONCEPTIONS OF THE CAMERA AND SOME CONSEQUENCES FOR A HISTORY OF NARRATIVE

Major Conceptions of the Camera	Theory of Narrative Meaning: How Are Present Entities Related to Absent Entities? i.e., A→B	Example of One Favored Camera Technique	One Major Value of Narrativity for Society	One Major Principle for the Writing of a History of Narrative
Camera as Origin of a Sensory Display (A Machine)	Illusion (e.g., of depth)	Kinetic Depth	Hallucinatory Involvement	Edison, Griffith (vs. Lumière, Méliès)
Camera as Sensory (or Material) Form	Defamiliarization	Unmotivated Camera	Art as Social and Political Tool	Pressure from an Avant-garde
Camera as Recorder of the Profilmic (An Act of Pointing)	Causal: the Physics of Light Rays	Deep Focus (Objective Camera)	Reproduction of Visible, Unobtrusive Reality	Lumière (vs. Méliès)
Camera as Agent for a Postfilmic Viewing Situation	*BAZINIAN THEORY* Perceiver Sees A as He or She *Would See* B (subjunctive conditional)	Lateral Depth of Field	Reproduction of Human Perception at Work	Renoir, Welles; Neorealism
Camera as Expressive of Bodily and Mental States	Intention	Subjective Camera	Celebration of the Individual and the Inner World	The Auteur
Camera as Channel for Communication	Causal: Signal Transmission	Personification of the Camera (= narrator's presence objectified)	Information	Art Cinema
Camera as Fantasy	Unconscious Mechanisms	Visualization of Dream-Thought ('representability')	Visual Pleasure and the Dynamic of the Repressed	Classical Cinema
Camera as Semantic Label	Symbol	?	The World as Text	Types of Reference: Filmic and Nonfilmic Codes; Reading

NOTES

1. André Bazin. *What is Cinema?*, 2 vols., trans. Hugh Gray (Los Angeles, CA: University of California Press, 1967 [Vol. I], 1971 [Vol. II]).
To my knowledge, the nature of a camera has been directly addressed by only two authors. Irving Pichel argues that the camera is a mixture of several of the conceptions I describe, while David Bordwell demonstrates, in a very instructive way, the incompleteness of profilmic and perceptual accounts of the camera: Irving Pichel, 'Seeing with the Camera,' *Hollywood Quarterly*, vol. 1, no. 2 (1946), pp. 138-145 (reprinted in *Hollywood Directors 1941-1976*, ed. Richard Koszarski [New York: Oxford University Press, 1977], pp. 69-81, also reprinted as 'Change of Camera Viewpoint,' in *The Movies as Medium*, ed. Lewis Jacobs [New York: Farrar, Straus & Giroux, 1970], pp. 113-123); and David Bordwell, 'Camera Movement and Cinematic Space,' *Ciné-Tracts*, vol. 1, no. 2 (1977), pp. 19-25.
I wish to thank Roberta Kimmel for her editorial assistance and Kristin Thompson, Dudley Andrew and Janet Staiger for their helpful comments on this paper.

2. In concentrating on the notion of the camera, I do not imply that it is the most important fact about film, but merely that it is one fact about film and a convenient starting point. In addition, there are a number of issues I will not address. I will avoid asking evaluative questions, such as what makes camerawork elegant, subtle, powerful, ineffective, poor, clumsy, etc. I will not explicitly discuss the various theories of subjectivity (involving authorship, narration, theory of character and the act of viewing) which arise from different conceptions of the camera; nor will I discuss materialist and idealist versions of each conception. The eight conceptions of the camera which I do discuss in what follows are not meant to be an exhaustive list; consider, for example, Manuel De Landa's interesting application of Wittgenstein's theory of language to film, 'Wittgenstein at the Movies,' (in this volume, pp. 108-119). How would such a theory conceive of the camera? Finally, I will largely avoid criticism of the different conceptions of the camera because to do so opens a vast territory which may, at any rate, be relatively familiar to the reader.

3. For general comment on the problem of meaning see Richard Wollheim, 'Representation: The Philosophical Contribution to Psychology,' *Critical Inquiry*, vol. 3, no. 4 (1977), pp. 709-723.

4. The diagram is taken from Ulric Neisser, 'The Processes of Vision,' in *Perception: Mechanisms and Models*, ed. Richard Held and Whitman Richards (San Francisco, CA: W.H. Freeman, 1972), pp. 252-259; originally published in *Scientific American*, vol. 219, no. 3 (1968), p. 210.

5. In saying that the camera is the 'simplest hypothesis' a spectator can make about certain perceptual arrays, I avoid saying it is a 'necessary' hypothesis. Not all movements ascribed to a camera are the result of movement by a camera, and conversely, not all movements by a camera produce a perception of camera movement. Camerawork, like editing, involves the perception of

form through successive, partial views, and such perception involves rather complex sensory processes. See Irvin Rock, 'Anorthoscopic Perception,' *Scientific American*, vol. 244, no. 3 (1981), pp. 145-153.

6. Percepts are fully 'real' to an individual, and the perceptual processes on which they are based can be described scientifically. What is 'illusory' is the fact that percepts can be produced artificially without guaranteeing the actual presence of that which is perceived. Typically the processes studied are more complex than the retinal image produced by an object but less complex than higher order cognitive functions. It is well-accepted that an accurate retinal image of a display is neither necessary nor sufficient to explain perception. On the other hand, the appearance, say, of an optical illusion is not altered by the fact that we 'know' it to be an illusion; it retains its power even in the face of disbelief and rational explanation. One seemingly cannot argue with an illusion. This irresistible nature of illusion accounts for the negative judgements of it made by such writers as Plato and Brecht.

7. E.H. Gombrich, 'Illusion and Art,' in *Illusion in Nature and Art*, ed. R.L. Gregory and E.H. Gombrich (New York: Charles Scribner's Sons, 1973), pp. 192-243 ('. . . our problem is precisely to what extent art may elicit phantom perceptions' [p. 212, see also p. 208]; on cinema, see pp. 240-241); Jean-Louis Baudry, 'The Apparatus,' trans. Jean Andrews and Bertrand Augst, *Camera Obscura*, no. 1 (1976), pp. 104-126.

8. Noël Burch, *To the Distant Observer* (Los Angeles, CA: University of California Press, 1979), chap. 20, passim; Noël Burch and Jorge Dana, 'Propositions,' trans. Diana Matias and Christopher King, *Afterimage*, no. 5 (1974), pp. 40-67.
Though Burch in *To the Distant Observer* does not spell out what constitutes 'gratuitous' camera movement (p. 222), the concept is relatively familiar and refers to camera movement which is *not* motivated by diegetic (i.e., illusory) space and time; more precisely, it performs some function *other* than the following:

    (1) to establish scenographic space

    (2) to follow or anticipate movement by a character or object

    (3) to follow or discover a glance

    (4) to select a narratively significant detail (e.g., an inserted dolly shot of an object or facial expression)

    (5) to reveal character subjectivity

Unmotivated camera movement is evidence of an activity of framing which lags behind or else searches out narrative detail; that is, it is evidence of imperfect knowledge. However, for some textual systems it may also be interpreted either as a pure effect of narration or sometimes as an independent, non-narrative system within the text. For analyses utilizing this latter concept see David Bordwell, *The Films of Carl-Theodor Dreyer* (Los Angeles, CA: University of California Press, 1981), pp. 153-164 (on *Ordet*); and Brian Henderson, 'Toward a Non-Bourgeois Camera Style,' *Film Quarterly*, vol. 24, no. 2 (1970-1971), pp. 2-14 (on *Weekend*). See also note 14.

9. Burch, 'A Parenthesis on Film History,' in *To the Distant Observer*, chap. 5, and 'Porter, or Ambivalence,' trans. Tom Milne, *Screen*, vol. 19, no. 4 (1978-1979), pp. 91-105.
It is often claimed that exploration of non-illusionist aspects of film falls to the avant-garde; see, for example, Grahame Weinbren and Christine Brinckmann, 'Selective Transparencies:. Pat O'Neill's Recent Films,' *Millennium Film Journal*, no. 6 (1980), pp. 50-72.

10. Michael Baxandall, *Painting and Experience in Fifteenth Century Italy* (Oxford: Clarendon Press, 1972), pp. 40-45. According to the Church, illusionist painting fostered piety because it was more direct, emotional and lasting. It also did not require literacy. On the relation of Renaissance perspective to cinema see William Wees, 'The Cinematic Image as a Visualization of Sight,' *Wide Angle*, vol. 4, no. 3 (1980), pp. 28-37.

11. Noël Burch, *Theory of Film Practice*, trans. Helen Lane (1973; rpt. Princeton, NJ: Princeton University Press, 1981).

12. On defamiliarization in film see Kristin Thompson, *Eisenstein's 'Ivan the Terrible': A Neoformalist Analysis* (Princeton, NJ: Princeton University Press, 1981), especially chap. 1, 'A Neoformalist Method of Film Criticism.'

13. Dana Polan, 'Formalism and its Discontents,' *Jump Cut*, no. 26 (1981), p. 65.

14. Sergei M. Eisenstein, 'The Cinematographic Principle and the Ideogram,' in *Film Form*, trans. Jay Leyda (New York: Harcourt, Brace & World, 1949), p. 41. Unmotivated camera movement is one instance of an obtrusive camera. See also note 8.

15. Bazin, 'The Ontology of the Photographic Image,' in *What is Cinema?*, vol. I, p. 15.

16. Arthur Danto, 'Moving Pictures,' *Quarterly Review of Film Studies*, vol. 4, no. 1 (1979), p. 19.

17. Roger Scruton, 'Photography and Representation,' *Critical Inquiry*, vol. 7, no. 3 (1981), pp. 589, 598-603. Scruton asserts that 'The camera . . . is being used not to represent something but to point to it. The subject [i.e., the object pointed to], once located, plays its own special part in an independent process of representation. The camera is not essential to that process: a gesturing finger would have served just as well.' Scruton goes on to repeat that well-worn assertion that the camera may on occasion be used for interest, emphasis and 'peculiar effects of atmosphere.' Again, the camera is deemed radically external to a dramatic *mise-en-scène* and hence, for Scruton, incidental. Compare Rudolf Arnheim's view that cinema is truly art only insofar as it can escape photographic realism (*Film as Art* [Los Angeles, CA: University of California Press, 1957]). See also note 38.

18. Scruton, p. 594.

19. André Bazin, 'William Wyler ou le janseniste de la mise-en-scène,' *Qu'est-ce que le cinéma?*, vol. I (Paris: Editions du Cerf, 1958), p. 157 (emphasis mine). See also Dudley Andrew, 'Realism and Reality in Cinema: The Film Theory of André Bazin and Its Source in Recent French Thought' (Ph. D. Dissertation, University of Iowa, 1972), pp. 82-93.

20. André Bazin, *Orson Welles: A Critical View*, trans. Jonathan Rosenbaum (New York: Harper & Row, 1978), p. 77.

21. Karel Reisz and Gavin Millar, *The Technique of Film Editing*, 2nd ed. (New York: Hastings House, 1968), pp. 249, 255. See generally Hugo Munsterberg, *The Film: A Psychological Study* (1916; rpt. New York: Dover Publications, 1970), and Gerard Buckle, *The Mind and the Film* (1926; rpt. New York: Arno Press, 1970).

22. Ernest Lindgren, *The Art of the Film* (New York: Collier Books, 1963), pp. 158, 166.

23. Reisz and Millar, pp. 233-236.

24. Ibid., pp. 213, 215. See also notes 19, 20, 29, and Lindgren, pp. 65-67.

25. 'Lateral depth of field' is a type of camera movement which results in the 'almost total disappearance of montage.' Bazin describes it as follows: 'Since what we are shown is only significant in terms of what is hidden from us and since therefore the value of what we see is continually threatened, the *mise-en-scène* cannot limit itself to what is presented on the screen. The rest of the scene, while effectively hidden, should not cease to exist. . . . The camera should be able to spin suddenly without picking up any holes or dead spots in the action.

'What all of this means is that the scene should be played independent of the camera in all its real dramatic expanse and that it is up to the cameraman to let his viewfinder play over the action. Reframing, then, is substituted as much as possible for a switching of points of view, which not only introduces spatial discontinuity, a phenomenon foreign to the nature of the human eye, but also sanctions the concept of the reality of a shot on a single plane, the idea of each shot as nothing more than a unit of place and action, an atom which joins with other atoms to make the scene and then the sequence.' (André Bazin, *Jean Renoir*, trans. W.W. Halsey II and William Simon [New York: Dell Publishing, 1973], p. 89.)

26. See note 25. Bazin restricts the independence of the camera in a number of ways. Its mobility and vision are confined to what an invisible witness (who is curious but not perfect) *would see* under identical conditions. Thus not all 'unmotivated' camera movements (see note 8) will qualify. (*Jean Renoir*, pp. 87-91; see also, 'Theater and Cinema, Part Two,' in *What is Cinema?*, vol. I, pp. 102-107.)

27. A weaker claim is sometimes advanced which asserts that film places the spectator only at a scene *as if* it were actually being played *on a stage*. This claim attempts to strike a compromise between a film's apparent twin sources in real space and fictional space, but only succeeds in postponing the problem: What is the nature of a stage play? There is no ontological halfway house. Note that these formulations of the nature of meaning involve statements in the subjunctive conditional mood. Some of the difficulties in analyzing statements in this mood are explored by A.J. Ayer, *Probability and Evidence* (New York: Macmillan Co., 1972), pp. 111-139; and Nelson Goodman, *Fact, Fiction, and Forecast*, 3rd ed. (Indianapolis, IN: Hackett Publishing Co., 1977).

28. For Bazin, the 'facts' of reality are always prior to, and distinct from, 'meaning.' Thus he shares the mystic's belief that there exists a knowledge not expressible in a semantic system (through words, pictures, gestures, etc.). This sort of experience is either prior to language (in the broadest sense) or beyond language. ('Le Réalisme cinématographique et l'école italienne de la libération,' in *Qu'est-ce que le cinéma?*, vol. IV, p. 34; and 'An Aesthetic of Reality: Neorealism,' in *What is Cinema?*, vol. II, pp. 28, 35-38.)

Bazin argues that the inherent reality of film responds to an individual's fear of death by promising to preserve life through photography's unique power to 'embalm' time. ('The Ontology of The Photographic Image,' in *What is Cinema?*, vol. I, pp. 9-16.) In this way, as Philip Rosen has pointed out to me, Bazin's theory of representation becomes immersed in theological values.

29. Kenneth Roberts and Win Sharples argue that camera movement must be unobtrusive in order to duplicate human perception: 'In the proper hands movement of the camera can be a powerful means of visual expression, but the secret to its success is in the ability to move without calling attention to the movement. This can be achieved by having the camera's movement resemble the physical and mental experiences of human vision. When the camera is moved so as to capture these experiences, the spectator will accept such movement because he is unaware of it.' (Kenneth Roberts and Win Sharples, *A Primer for Filmmaking* [Indianapolis, IN: Pegasus, 1971], p. 102; see also pp. 102-107, 132-134.)

30. See Gerald Mast, 'Kracauer's Two Tendencies and the Early History of Film Narrative,' *Critical Inquiry*, vol. 6, no. 3 (1980), pp. 475-476.

31. Bazin, *Jean Renoir*, pp. 84-85, 105-106. See also his 'Theater and Cinema, Part Two,' in *What is Cinema?*, vol. I, p. 110; and 'The Evolution of the Language of the Cinema,' ibid., pp. 23-40.

32. See Bazin's analysis of *The River*—a film which eschews the favored techniques yet, he claims, is unsurpassed in its realism (in *Jean Renoir*, chap. 8).

33. On the perfect view convention, see my 'Subjectivity Under Siege—From Fellini's *8 1/2* to Oshima's *The Story of a Man Who Left His Will on Film*,' *Screen*, vol. 19, no. 1 (1978), pp. 28-29.

34. Ernest Lindgren states that 'Camera movement . . . very often carries with it a certain subjective impression. The movement of the camera draws attention to the *imaginary observer* whose movement it reproduces. The content of the shot is seen, not directly, but through the eyes, as it were, of someone who is *reacting to* that content in a certain way.' (Lindgren, p. 164 [emphasis mine].)

35. A useful summary of some issues involving expression theories is F.E. Sparshott, 'Goodman

on Expression,' *The Monist*, vol. 58, no. 2 (1974), pp. 187-202. On the ideology of Romanticism see Tzvetan Todorov, 'The Romantic Crisis,' in *Theories of the Symbol*, trans. Catherine Porter (Oxford: Basil Blackwell, 1982), pp. 147-221.

36. The popular assertion that film 'reflects,' 'mirrors' or is a 'window' onto the world or onto the soul is really no explanation at all. Related concepts, such as likeness, resemblance, copy and mimesis are scarcely better. See, for example, Nelson Goodman, *Languages of Art: An Approach to a Theory of Symbols*, 2nd ed. (Indianapolis, IN: Hackett Publishing Co., 1976), pp. 3-19; and Max Black, 'How Do Pictures Represent?', in *Art, Perception, and Reality* (Baltimore, MD: Johns Hopkins University Press, 1970), pp. 95-130.

37. Rudolf Arnheim, 'The Gestalt Theory of Expression,' in *Toward a Psychology of Art* (Los Angeles, CA: University of California Press, 1966). Various expressive theories are combined by Béla Balázs, *Theory of the Film: Character and Growth of a New Art*, trans. Edith Bone (1945; rpt. New York: Dover Publications, 1970), especially chap. 9.

38. Alexandre Astruc, 'The Birth of a New Avant-garde: La Caméra-stylo,' in *The New Wave*, ed. Peter Graham (New York: Doubleday & Co., 1968), pp. 17-23. The paintbrush metaphor for the camera is quite common. Since it is based on an expressive theory of meaning, it can lead, paradoxically, to the judgement that the camera is actually more machine than creative instrument. (Virgil Aldrich, *Philosophy of Art* [Englewood Cliffs, NJ: Prentice-Hall, 1963], pp. 62-63.) See also note 17.

39. Andrew Sarris, *The American Cinema: Directors and Directions, 1929-1968* (New York: E.P. Dutton, 1968), pp. 269-300; see also his introduction, 'Toward a Theory of Film History,' pp. 19-37.

40. Hayden White, 'The Value of Narrativity in the Representation of Reality,' *Critical Inquiry*, vol. 7, no. 1 (1980), p. 5; Victor Turner, 'Social Dramas and Stories About Them,' ibid., p. 167.

41. Umberto Eco, 'Signification and Communication,' in *A Theory of Semiotics* (Bloomington, IN: Indiana University Press, 1976), pp. 32-47; James Kinneavy, 'Comprehensive Theory of the Field of English,' in *A Theory of Discourse: The Aims of Discourse* (New York: W.W. Norton, 1971), pp. 17-40; Seymour Chatman, *Story and Discourse: Narrative Structure in Fiction and Film* (Ithaca, NY: Cornell University Press, 1978), pp. 146-161.

42. Roman Jakobson, 'Linguistics and Poetics,' in *The Structuralists: From Marx to Lévi-Strauss*, ed. Richard and Fernande de George (Garden City, NY: Anchor Books, 1972), pp. 89, 92.

43. Nick Browne, 'The Spectator-in-the-Text: The Rhetoric of *Stagecoach*,' *Film Quarterly*, vol. 29, no. 2 (1975-1976), p. 26. See also his 'Film Form/Voice-Over: Bresson's *The Diary of a Country Priest*,' *Yale French Studies*, no. 60 (1980), pp. 234.

44. Dudley Andrew, 'The Gravity of *Sunrise*,' *Quarterly Review of Film Studies*, vol. 2, no. 3 (1977), p. 370 (village); Bruce Kawin, *Mindscreen: Bergman, Godard, and First-Person Film* (Princeton, NJ: Princeton University Press, 1978), pp. 173, 181, 183 (Paris); Browne, 'The Spectator-in-the-Text,' p. 35 (character Lucy); Browne, 'Film Form,' pp. 233, 237 (the priest); Tony Pipolo, 'The Aptness of Terminology: Point of View, Consciousness and *Letter From An Unknown Woman*,' *Film Reader*, no. 4 (1979), pp. 167, 169, 171 (character Lisa); Browne, 'Narrative Point of View: The Rhetoric of *Au Hasard, Balthazar*,' *Film Quarterly*, vol. 31, no. 1 (1977), pp. 29-31 (donkey); Kawin, pp. 93, 135, 139 (God); ibid., pp. 56, 106 (arc rods of a projector); ibid., pp. 3, 17, 56, 92, passim (mind of the film text itself).

45. Andrew, '*Sunrise*,' p. 362; Bazin, *Jean Renoir*, p. 87; James McLaughlin, 'All in the Family: Alfred Hitchcock's *Shadow of a Doubt*,' *Wide Angle*, vol. 4, no. 1 (1980), p. 13; William Rothman, 'Alfred Hitchcock's *Murder!*: Theater, Authorship and the Presence of the Camera,' *Wide Angle*, vol. 4, no. 1 (1980), p. 60; Danto, 'Moving Pictures,' p. 19; Raymond Durgnat, 'The Restless Camera,' *Films and Filming*, vol. 15, no. 3 (1968), p. 15.
Tony Pipolo declares that 'the correspondences between character and camera "behavior"

amount to this: the camera is personified to the degree that it acts in unison with, and often as a substitute for, the character consciousness which controls it.' ('The Aptness of Terminology,' p. 172.)

46. David Bordwell, 'The Art Cinema as a Mode of Film Practice,' *Film Criticism*, vol. 4, no. 1 (1979), especially pp. 59-61; Steve Neale, 'Art Cinema as Institution,' *Screen*, vol. 22, no. 1 (1981), pp. 11-39.

47. See Freud's analysis of the enactment of presence and absence in the child's game of *Fort/Da*, in *Beyond the Pleasure Principle* (London: International Psycho-Analytical Press, 1922), pp. 11-16. See also Walter Benjamin's suggestive phrase, 'unconscious optics,' in 'The Work of Art in the Age of Mechanical Reproduction,' in *Illuminations*, trans. Harry Zohn (New York: Schocken Books, 1969), pp. 235-237.

48. Jean-Louis Baudry, 'The Apparatus'; Laura Mulvey, 'Visual Pleasure and Narrative Cinema,' *Screen*, vol. 16, no. 3 (1975), especially pp. 13, 17-18.

49. The dream process in which the camera plays a role is known as 'considerations of representability.' See J. Laplanche and J.-B. Pontalis, *The Language of Psycho-Analysis*, trans. Donald Nicholson-Smith (New York: W.W. Norton, 1973), pp. 389-390. Other processes of dream-work include condensation, displacement and secondary revision. For a bibliography on cinema as a dream, see *Dreamworks*, vol. 1, no. 1 (1980).

Another important psychological process is identification, and leads to the concept of a spectator's 'identification with the camera.' See Christian Metz, 'The Imaginary Signifier,' trans. Ben Brewster, *Screen*, vol. 16, no. 2 (1975), pp. 52-54.

50. 'The most striking example here is perhaps the literalism, i.e., the literal production in the filmic text of a verbal metaphor in *Le Plaisir*. As a joke—and it is interesting that he should have chosen to say it in this way—Ophuls explained that the reason for the convoluted crane movement along the walls of the brothel in the *Maison Tellier* episode, peering through windows but never cutting to the inside of the house, was because the Maison Tellier was precisely a *maison close*, a closed house. Behind its doors and windows is locked away what a rigorous social morality excludes from its legal order. So the camera is on the side of the Law, *but it is the repressed* (here the repression of the verbal term combined with the inscription of socio-sexual repression) *which moves it along*, obsessively circling its object of fascination, describing in its movement the outlines of the gaps in the social fabric, catching glimpses of the forbidden areas, but from the outside.' (Paul Willemen, 'The Ophuls Text: A Thesis,' in *Ophuls*, ed. Paul Willemen [London: British Film Institute, 1978], pp. 70-71 [emphasis mine]).

Further details of what Willemen terms a 'literalism' may be found in Willemen, 'Cinematic Discourse—The Problem of Inner Speech,' *Screen*, vol. 22, no. 3 (1981), pp. 63-93 (reprinted in *Cinema and Language*, ed. Stephen Heath and Patricia Mellencamp [Los Angeles, CA: The American Film Institute, 1983], pp. 141-167); and his 'Reflections on Eikhenbaum's Concept of Internal Speech in the Cinema,' *Screen*, vol. 15, no. 4 (1974-1975), pp. 59-70; and 'The Fugitive Subject,' in *Raoul Walsh*, ed. Phil Hardy (Edinburgh: Edinburgh Film Festival, 1974), pp. 62-89. For criticism, see Noël Carroll, 'Language and Cinema: Preliminary Notes for a Theory of Verbal Images,' *Millennium Film Journal*, nos. 7/8/9 (1980-1981), pp. 186-217. See generally Roy Schafer, 'Action and Narration in Psychoanalysis,' *New Literary History*, vol. 12, no. 1 (1980), pp. 61-85.

51. See, for example, Mulvey, 'Visual Pleasure.' Phallic aggression is depicted literally in *King Kong* (1933). The heroine rehearses terrified reactions as the camera becomes King Kong by assuming in advance the creature's place. In Frank Borzage's *Liliom* (1930) the subordination of the female gaze is depicted literally when, in a scene involving a wedding portrait, a bride is told to look at her husband while he is told to look into the lens of the camera. The first example is from Thierry Kuntzel, 'Lecture on King Kong' (University of Wisconsin-Madison, Spring, 1976).

52. Metz, 'The Imaginary Signifier,' pp. 28, 35-36, 54-55.

53. A starting point is the early work of Christian Metz. See his *Language and Cinema*, trans. Donna Jean Umiker-Sebeok (The Hague: Mouton, 1974); and *Film Language: A Semiotics of the Cinema*, trans. Michael Taylor (New York: Oxford University Press, 1974).

54. See Alain Robbe-Grillet, 'Nature, Humanism, Tragedy,' in *For a New Novel: Essays on Fiction*, trans. Richard Howard (New York: Grove Press, 1965), pp. 49-75.

55. See Roland Barthes, 'The Structuralist Activity,' in *Critical Essays*, trans. Richard Howard (Evanston, IL: Northwestern University Press, 1972), p. 219.

56. Metz, *Film Language*, pp. 113, 143-145.

57. See David Bordwell, 'Imploded Space: Film Style in *The Passion of Jeanne d'Arc*,' in *Purdue Film Studies*, vol. 1 (Pleasantville, NY: Redgrave Publishing), especially pp. 102-104.

58. Hitchcock's description of the shot can be found in François Truffaut, *Hitchcock* (New York: Simon & Schuster, 1967), pp. 186-187.

59. Arnheim also makes stronger claims about the importance of gravity in the perception of forms. (Rudolf Arnheim, *Art and Visual Perception*, 2nd ed. [Los Angeles, CA: University of California Press, 1974], pp. 23-24, 30-32, 101-103, 184-187; and *The Dynamics of Architectural Form* [Los Angeles, CA: University of California Press, 1977], chap. 2.) See also Irvin Rock, 'The Perception of Disoriented Figures,' *Scientific American*, vol. 230, no. 1 (1974), pp. 78-85.

60. I have elaborated on the notion of the camera as viewing hypothesis in 'The Spectator and Film Space—Two Theories,' *Screen*, vol. 22, no. 1 (1981), pp. 55-78; and in 'Narration,' in my *Point of View in the Cinema: A Theory of Narration and Subjectivity in Classical Film* (New York: Mouton, 1984), chap. 3.

Wittgenstein at the Movies

Manuel De Landa

The purpose of this paper is to analyze certain linguistic skills displayed by audiences when they are engaged in watching a narrative film and in particular their ability to ascribe beliefs to characters on the screen. The exploitation of this skill, it will be argued, plays a key role in the process of getting the audience involved in the plot. But before setting out to explore our subject I would like to make some introductory remarks concerning my position regarding the nature of film theory.

In the first place, I believe that any film theory is parasitic upon a particular account of meaning. That is to say that any statement concerning the mechanisms of film is only true or false relative to the body of knowledge which constitutes that account of meaning. Outside of this relationship, statements about the functioning of films are simply nonsense.

This assertion might seem false to some and only trivially true to others. I ask those who disagree with it to wait for another discussion when I will have time to qualify it. To those who think that it is true but only trivially so—that is to say, that the assertion is true but that nothing of any importance follows from it—I hope to show some of the methodological consequences entailed by the logical dependence which film theories maintain with respect to philosophical, linguistic, psychological or even cybernetic accounts of meaning.

That this essential parasitism is not generally acknowledged can be seen in the very form in which some film theoreticians attack rival schools. To take only two examples, psychoanalytically-oriented theorists, concerned as they are with the relation between language and the genesis of subjectivity, will tend to reject accounts of film in which the subject of speech is taken for granted and never questioned. The philosophically or analytically-oriented theoretician, content with a definition of a human as a rule-following animal, will argue against using notions such as that of the unconscious on the grounds that such ghostly entities are not necessary to account for the audience's relation to movies. These theoreticians seem to be attacking one another as if they were engaged in explaining the same phenomenon, when in fact they are not. Film as an object of discourse is so elusive that our very notion of what it is that we are talking about depends on our conception of language and communication.[1]

One of the main practical effects of acknowledging this dependence is that we free ourselves to choose the descriptive method that best suits our purposes. Since any description of the mechanisms of film will highlight certain aspects of their functioning at the expense of others, one should always keep in mind that the apparent success that an approach has had in one area does not make it equally effective in other areas.

My purpose here is to try to describe the relation between viewer and film in a way that emphasizes the active role the spectator plays not only in making sense out of the film but, more importantly, in getting involved in the plot. Accordingly, I will choose an account of meaning that will permit me to define the consumption of narrative films as an active process; and of all the accounts that allow this I will choose the one that permits the most detailed definition of this process. To use a metaphor from optics: if a given descriptive system could be said to have more resolution in one area than in others, I will choose the method with maximum resolution in the area of my concern.

So, having established my methodological premises, I now return to the question: What is it that the spectator does when he or she ascribes a particular belief to a character on the screen? Say that a certain character is about to commit a crime motivated by his belief that his brother has been murdered by the person he's about to kill. Imagine also that we know his brother is alive and well. What is it that we do when we ascribe to him this false belief? Our answer will depend on our conception of the role that the verb 'believe' plays in our daily lives.

In the most traditional answer to this question, to say of somebody that he or she has a belief is to refer to a certain mental state of the believer. There is a wide variety of interpretations as to how the belief in question is stored in the brain, but all of them seem to argue that a belief is some kind of psychological state. Let's call this approach the mentalist account. For reasons that I will shortly put forward, this account does not provide the amount of detail that I need to apply it to film.

An alternative account could be found in the analysis that Gilbert Ryle offers of what he calls dispositional verbs. According to this theory, to say that somebody has a belief is not to refer to a mental act but to produce an open set of hypothetical sentences which describe how the believer would tend to act in certain circumstances. To use Ryle's classic example: a gardener's belief that it will rain does not consist in his being in a particular state of mind, but in the *form* of his *behavior*—he keeps his coat handy, leaves the watering-can in the tool shed, beds out more seedlings, and so on. This belief, far from being a private mental entity, is embodied in the shape in which he practices his gardening skills. And to say that he believes it is going to rain is to *produce* an open set of sentences describing those actions and an indefinite number of kindred ones.[2] However, not only are verbs such as 'believe' (which signify tendencies) dispositional, but also verbs such as 'know' (which signify capabilities). To say that a person knows something is not to say that he or she is at a particular moment in the process of doing or undergoing anything, but that he or she is able to do certain things when the need arises, or that he or she is prone to do and feel certain things in certain kinds of situations.

As it happens, most of the personality traits that define a character in a narrative film, and not only his or her beliefs and knowledge, could be construed as dispositions. These dispositions vary in many respects, but most importantly in the number of *kinds* of behaviors that they make us expect from the character to whom we attribute them. For example, when we know that a character is a compulsive cigarette smoker, we construct a relatively small set of hypotheticals containing sentences such as: 'If he did not have any cigarettes, he would feel nervous.' However, if we attribute to the character the quality of being, say, clever or vain, the open set of hypotheticals is much bigger because the number of actions through which those qualities are *displayed* is indefinite.

Now I can explain why the mentalist account seemed to me insufficient for describing in necessary detail the practice of watching a narrative film. Even if attributing beliefs in everyday life is to refer to an event or a state in the believer's mind, characters in a movie certainly do not have minds; therefore, all that the audience would be doing in attributing to characters such states of mind would be *pretending* to do so. That is to say, the audience, in this account, appears as a group of people willing to participate in a game of make-believe, some kind of ritual suspension of disbelief. The audience would assume that a character is *supposed* to have belief insofar as such an assumption is important in order to follow the plot.

Now, for some purposes, say for an analysis of use to an advertising agency, this account might suffice. To me it seems that the mentalist account, at least in the form outlined, only explains the spectator's ability to follow the plot. It does not explain the fact that, in following the plot, the spectator can become engaged in the characters' lives, might care about their fates, or might desire intensively the worst possible future for them (e.g., 'J.R., the man you love to hate').

A dispositional account of narrative film indicates that to establish the traits that define a character is to engage the audience in the *production of possible worlds*, one for each character. That is to say, the open sets of hypothetical sentences that establish how a character is expected to behave in different circumstances would create a world of possible actions for each character. This is an active practice of producing worlds that would endow characters with that minimum of life necessary for us to relate to them erotically—either to love them or to hate them. In the same way that following a tune involves not only hearing the notes but also having the proper niche ready for each note as it comes, getting involved with the plot of a movie involves the production of a network of niches for possible actions and reactions of the characters. The relative credibility of a plot would depend, from this point of view, on how much it respects the rules that govern this network of niches. In other words, as we form expectations about the characters' future behavior, we create *criteria* that the plot must meet in order to remain believable.

The question of why the audience demands that a plot must be believable can be answered by a parallel with ordinary language. In everyday language situations, certain unstated conversational maxims operate.[3] One of them, for example, dictates that we relate to our interlocutor as if he or she were trying to make sense; even though it is perfectly imaginable that people might go around talking nonsense, we regularly assume they do not. In a similar way, audiences of commercial movies grew to expect from films, at least within certain genres, that their plots would try to make sense. Movies that did not comply with this maxim were labeled experimental, avant-garde, and so forth, and consumed in a different way. A borderline case could be an average spectator watching an early French New Wave film and being so confused as to how he or she is *supposed* to consume the film that he or she in the end feels cheated by the plot.

A final parallel will help to round out the picture I have presented of the way in which audiences consume narrative films. The function of a snapshot is to induce in a person the ability to picture the object whose visible likeness has been encoded by the lens. Similarly, a narrative film would work by inducing in the audience the ability to perceive a series of such likenesses *as forming situations* and as tracing more or less plausible lines of development for the plot. That is to say, if a still picture stimulates me to *seem to perceive* the photographed situation, a narrative film stimulates me to seem to live those situations.[4] In short, what I mean to say is that a competent commercial film, a film with relatively achieved characterizations and a coherent plot, by engaging the audience in the production of possible worlds, creates a situation that permits the audience to inhabit those worlds.

It is my belief that Wittgenstein's use theory of meaning yields maximum resolution in this particular area of film theory. This is most evident in that area of his theory that lends itself to formal analysis, namely the theory of speech acts. Speech acts are actions performed through the use of language, such as promises, bets, warnings, and so forth.[5] Most speech acts performed on the screen are regarded by the audience as involving the characters in situations and commitments similar to those in which real people become involved. Once a speech act has been performed on the screen, any failure on the characters' part to act appropriately will only undermine the relative credibility of the plot. A promise, an order, a warning, as well as any other speech act, has certain conditions that must be met in order for the act to be valid. Most moviegoers would not be able to describe those conditions but would be capable of spotting a situation in real life where those conditions have not been met. We learn to recognize these situations before we can learn to describe them or to picture them (i.e., to seem to perceive them). The ability to picture performance conditions for speech acts is greatly enhanced by narrative films. But this is possible only because audiences are already linguistically equipped to identify those conditions in real life.

In all of this I have not yet mentioned the reasons I consider the use theory of meaning as particularly well-suited for the study of the processes of consumption of narrative films. In order to discuss this, I would like to move to a more abstract plane and compare a Wittgensteinian approach with the account of language that prevails in most semiological analysis of film today, namely, that of continental linguistics. I think that the differences and similarities of the two approaches illustrate very clearly a central premise of this paper: that there is at least one film theory per account of meaning.

To review the similarities first, we may draw on the formulation of continental linguistics as summarized by Emile Benveniste.[6] His formulation is useful for us here because in it he explicitly compares his approach with those of logicians and analytical philosophers. In Benveniste's view, language is structured along two axes: the paradigmatic, which he calls the semiotic level, and the syntagmatic, which he calls the semantic level. At the semiotic level there are only differences. Language appears as a closed system of signs in which the property of being meaningful is accounted for by those signs standing in relations of opposition to one another. A sign is defined as the result of the bonding of a signified (a concept, an idea) and a signifier (a sound-image). Neither has any positive content in itself. Their contents are purely differential, defined by their relationships to other elements in the system. The semantic level, on the other hand, is the level of language actualized in real-life communication, of meaning as intended by a particular speaker. Here the units are no longer signs, but words combined in sentences. Relevant for us here is that Benveniste believes that all the traditional categories used in logic (i.e., the syntactic, the semantic and the pragmatic levels) refer to what he would call the semantic categories. He even goes so far as to suggest that the deep structure of transformational grammar is a semantic category. Thus what he wants to show by drawing the semiotic/semantic distinction is that Saussure discovers a completely new domain of language, the semiotic level—a domain of structural coexistences which escapes traditional analysis concentrated at the semantic level.

Here lies the most important similarity with Wittgenstein's approach. In the use theory of meaning, the emphasis is also placed on the systematic character of language. This is central to the famous private-language argument. In that argument, Wittgenstein attempts to prove that an individual is incapable of endowing a sign with meaning even if the sign supposedly refers to a private feeling, a feeling to which the individual alone has access. In a simplified version the argument runs as follows: I cannot propose to myself the definition: 'From now on this feeling is going to be called X,' because to do so would be like inventing for myself a rule in a game which is public. And if I did so, how could I know that I am following the rule since there are no independent criteria to establish whether I have made a mistake? Any use of the word X to refer to my feeling anything, if it seems correct to me, will count as a correct application of X. (To try to endow a sign with meaning in this form is like trying to push a car from the inside.)[7]

What matters to us here is that both in the semiotic, which we could also call the synchronic, and in the use accounts of meaning, the accent is put on the fact that signs exist as such only because they are connected to other signs. In the following passage, Saussure sounds very much like Wittgenstein:

> A community is necessary if linguistic values, that owe their existence solely to usage and general acceptance, are to be set up. By himself the individual is incapable of fixing a single value.[8]

The similarity is even more striking in the way both authors use the game of chess as a metaphor for language. Saussure considered it a fruitful simile because it illustrated how, just as the respective values of the chess pieces depend on their positions on the board, each linguistic term derives its value from its opposition to all other terms. In like manner, Wittgenstein repeatedly compares the meaning of a word to the role that a piece plays in a game, a role being defined by the rules that govern the game.

But if in this privilege given to the interconnections between signs lies the main similarity of the two approaches, in the conception of the nature of those interconnections lie even more important differences. To begin with, in continental linguistics the central idea is that of 'difference,' whereas in the use theory the key concept is the notion of 'criterion.' In the former, a sign, even if purely differential, still has a semantic core, the *idea* that the signifier stands for, namely the signified. In the latter, the signified as such disappears and the meaning of an expression is given by the criteria that specify its correct use. To put it differently, if in the former account a concept appears as a chunk of thought, in the latter it looks more like a recipe: it is a series of rules that define what has to be done with the signs and how this task is to be accomplished. In the use theory of meaning, to learn a word is not to receive generally valid information about what happens every time the sign is employed (in which case the sign stands for the same idea for everybody), but to learn to recognize the circumstances in which to *use* the sign properly. Learning the meaning of a word is treated as mastering a skill or acquiring an ability involving sensory-motor intelligence, and not just as establishing a connection between a sound and an *absent* object or concept. For Wittgenstein, then, the circumstances for the correct exercise of this skill are considered as part of the grammar of the language.

A second distinction between the two approaches concerns the nature of linguistic units. For Saussure both the signifier and the signified are psychological entities, arbitrarily held together in the brain by an associative bond. Thought is conceived as a shapeless and indistinct mass, an uncharted nebula, which is given form by language. Wittgenstein, on the contrary, could assert: 'One of the most dangerous ideas for a philosopher is, oddly enough, that we think with our heads or in our heads.' He always attacked the notion that the systematic relations which make up language are stored in the brain. As he puts it in *Zettel*:

> No supposition seems to me more natural than that there is *no* process in the brain correlated with associating or with thinking. So that it would be impossible to read off thought-processes from brain-processes. I mean this: if I talk or write there is, I assume, a system of impulses going out from my brain and correlated with my spoken or written thoughts. But why should the system continue further in the direction of the center? Why should this order not proceed, so to speak, out of chaos?[9]

Wittgenstein's distaste for what he calls 'the prejudice in favor of a psychological parallelism'[10] stems from his view of the process of learning a word as that of mastering a skill. It is conceivable that the information involved in and necessary to a skill is dispersed through the brain and the rest of the body; and also that it is embodied in the very form of the places where it is exercised, since a skill is not independent from the social site where it is practiced. An ability is always part of a series of discursive and non-discursive practices, and loses its meaning when isolated from the series. In short, what Wittgenstein does is to disperse the signified, which now becomes a function of the whole enunciation set-up. (This is where Wittgenstein departs from behaviorism: I could observe a behavior in an individual, but not a practice, which is always collective.)[11]

Regarding the signifier, there are also differences between the two thinkers. For Saussure the exemplary signifier is a sound-image, the 'psychological imprint' of sound-waves, whereas for Wittgenstein the signifier is always material. Wittgenstein's exemplary signifiers tend to be diagrams, charts, tables, labels, and so forth—entities which are physical embodiments of criteria. Consider, for example, the following passage:

> Imagine a man always carrying a sheet of paper in his pocket on which names of colors are coordinated with colored patches. You may say that it would be a nuisance to carry such a table of samples about with you, and that the mechanism of association is what we always use instead of it. But this is irrelevant; and in many cases it is not even true. . . . We could perfectly well, for our purposes, replace every process of imagining by a process of looking at an object or by painting, drawing or modelling; and every process of speaking to oneself by speaking aloud or by writing.[12]

It is clear that in Wittgenstein's account we can do without the mental counterparts of both physical sounds and images. For Saussure, on the contrary:

> The linguistic sign unites not a thing and a name, but a concept and a sound-image. The latter is not the material sound, a purely physical thing, but the psychological imprint of the sound, the impression that it makes on our senses. The sound image is sensory, and if I happen to call it 'material,' it is only in that sense. . . .[13]

In fact, I would argue that it is only in psychoanalysis, where the therapeutic (hence material) power of the word is fully exploited, that the Saussurian approach treats the signifier as being truly material.

This leads to a final difference between the two thinkers, one that concerns the logical nature of the bond between a sign and its meaning. In Saussure, this link is an arbitrary connection, for there is nothing inherent in the sound or the idea that would motivate their being linked. But once they become a sign, as Benveniste rightly stresses, the bond becomes necessary. A concept is a quality of its phonic substance, just as a particular slice of sound is a quality of the idea for which it stands.[14]

For Wittgenstein, on the other hand, this logical bond is a *criterial* relation. The criterial relation is weaker than that of the mutual entailment which holds together Saussure's signifier and signified. For example, in a basketball game a criterion for scoring is that the ball go through the hoop; however, the fact that it went through the hoop does not necessarily entail a score, because one of the rules of the game might have been broken.[15] A criterion is valid only with respect to the rest of the rules that make up a game. In language, the employment of words is governed by several criteria, since the conditions that justify their proper uses are always multiple. As Wittgenstein states:

> It characterizes the grammar of the proposition 'My finger moves, etc.'
> that I regard the propositions 'I see it move,' 'I feel it move,' 'He sees it
> move,' 'He tells me that it moves,' etc. as evidences for it.[16]

In other words, the set of propositions that I would count as criteria for the
proper use of an expression is always an open set. I could not enumerate all
the situations where the expression 'to think' would be adequately used,
although I might be able to recognize the wrong contexts as deviant ones. It
may well be impossible even to conceive of what a closed set of such criteria
would be like. So criteria never completely define the meaning of a word. For
every potential or actual use of a term of a language, there is a gentle
gradation from exceptions disregarded on trust, to hesitations over non-
applicability, to avoidances of the term as pointless.

Given the above comparison of the two approaches, I would like to
finish this paper by enumerating some of the relative advantages of each
approach when applied to the study of film.

With the discovery of the semiotic level, continental linguistics has
made possible the study of certain aspects of language with which analytical
philosophy is incapable of dealing. In particular, the differential account of
meaning allows us to pose the problem of the genesis of the subject in
language. This question has been addressed in the continental tradition even
outside of psychoanalysis, where it has always had the highest priority.
Benveniste himself gives us an interesting picture of how the subject is born
in language, arguing that it is the oppositional functioning of the personal
pronouns 'I-You' which permits the emergence of the human subject.[17]

When applied to film, this approach has enabled an emphasis on certain
structural determinations in the film-viewing situation which are involved in
the processes of transforming the viewing-subject into spectator. Again, it is
the differential conception of meaning that orients the research in the
direction of an analysis of the positioning operations which precede the
genesis of the film spectator. The perfect example is Metz' analysis of a
primary identification with the camera as an instance of discourse which
would be the basis for all the secondary, imaginary identifications with
particular characters.[18]

A criterial account of meaning in film theory, on the other hand, throws
light on an entirely different set of problems. As we saw, Wittgenstein's
move was to include the context of utterance in the grammar of a language, to
make linguistic skills and the institutional places for their exercise a
functional unity. And this unity was studied as a regulated set-up for the
production of meaning. The direction of this research is not towards defining
structurally determined positions but towards describing the multiplicity of
ways in which signs are used to create a world out of the sketchy information
that the film supplies.

The use theory is not the only account which would allow us to describe the film-viewing situation in this manner. But it does offer a rather unique perspective on the problem. Let us remember that in this account, learning the meaning of a word is not learning to associate a sound and a concept, but becoming capable of recognizing situations or scenes. This ability in turn is the basis for acquiring other skills, such as those of describing or picturing the situations or scenes. Part of what a film does is enhance our ability to picture scenes. Films can be highly elliptical because the spectator is continuously producing vivid pictures of situations out of the information with which he or she is presented. By showing that, as far as meaning is concerned, everything is essentially public, Wittgenstein helps us to explain how a medium like film, which captures only the external manifestations of thought and emotion, is capable of acquiring such high levels of verisimilitude.

In short, the use theory of meaning has situations (language-games) as its units; therefore, it seems particularly well-suited for describing a medium like film which consists, at least in its narrative use, of situations, and which demands from its audience the ability to get involved in those situations. I hope to have shown that this skill is only partially explained by an analysis in terms of positions and positioning mechanisms as in the semiotic approach, and that an account of the audience's labor in the production of possible worlds for the characters is necessary to give a more complete picture of the nature of narrative film.

NOTES

1. Notice that this assertion commits me to ontological relativism only with respect to theories of meaning. For an extension of this position to the physical sciences see Paul Feyerabend, *Against Method: Outline of an Anarchist Theory of Knowledge* (London: New Left Books, 1975).

Thanks to Joan Braderman, without whose discussion and criticism my ideas would be twice as imprecise.

2. Gilbert Ryle, *The Concept of Mind* (New York: Barnes & Noble, 1949), p. 133.

3. H.P. Grice, 'Logic and Conversation,' in *Syntax and Semantics*, vol. 3: *Speech Acts*, ed. Peter Cole and Jerry L. Morgan (New York: Academic Press, 1975), pp. 41-58.

4. Ryle, p. 254.

5. J.L. Austin, *How To Do Things With Words* (Cambridge, MA: Harvard University Press, 1962). I have here approached speech acts through examples of so-called performative utterances. But it should be noted that there is a complex controversy as to whether all speech acts are necessarily performative. In his book, Austin himself starts out by excluding assertions from the category of performatives. However, the distinction between constatives (assertions) and performatives (promises, bets, and so forth) gradually weakens as the book progresses, although Austin never quite gives it up. The problem is not central to my arguments here, so for the sake of brevity I have elided it.

Given the direction of my arguments, it may be relevant to note that speech acts form only a subclass of what Wittgenstein calls 'language games.' This latter category covers a much wider range of activities which are less semantically marked (asking favors, keeping secrets, for example) or less ritualized (lying, cheating) than Austin's speech acts. See Ludwig Wittgenstein, *Philosophical Investigations*, trans. G.E.M. Anscombe, 3rd ed. (New York: Macmillan Co., 1968), pp. 11-12, (no. 23).

6. See Emile Benveniste, 'La Forme et le sens dans le langage,' in *Problèmes de linguistique générale*, vol. II (Paris: Gallimard, 1974), pp. 215-238.

7. For an excellent treatment of this famous argument see Anthony Kenny, *Wittgenstein* (Cambridge, MA: Harvard University Press, 1973), chap. 10.

8. Ferdinand de Saussure, *Course in General Linguistics*, trans. Wade Baskin, ed. Charles Bally *et al.* (New York: McGraw-Hill, 1966), p. 113.

9. Ludwig Wittgenstein, *Zettel*, trans. G.E.M. Anscombe, ed. G.E.M. Anscombe and G.H. von Wright, 2nd ed. (Oxford: Basil Blackwell, 1981), pp. 104-106 (nos. 605-613; the quoted passages are from nos. 605 and 608). Wittgenstein would not want to deny, of course, that there is information stored in the brain. Rather, he rejects the idea that this information is a coded

version of a concept (signified) such that one could be derived from the other by using the proper rules of translation. One could read Wittgenstein, in the light of modern computer science, as saying that what this information specifies is an algorithm or recipe for producing the given concept in the proper context.

10. Wittgenstein, *Zettel*, p. 105 (no. 611).

11. Wittgenstein, *Philosophical Investigations*, p. 103 (no. 308; also nos. 310-311). See also Rush Rees, 'Questions of Logical Inference,' in *Understanding Wittgenstein*, ed. Godfrey N.A. Vesey (New York: St. Martin's Press, 1974).

12. Ludwig Wittgenstein, *The Blue and Brown Books*, 2nd ed. (New York: Harper & Row, 1968), p. 4.

13. Saussure, p. 66.

14. Emile Benveniste, 'The Nature of the Linguistic Sign,' in *Problems in General Linguistics*, trans. Mary Elizabeth Meek (Coral Gables, FL: University of Miami Press, 1971), pp. 43-49.

15. Peter M.S. Hacker, *Insight and Illusion: Wittgenstein on Philosophy and the Metaphysics of Experience* (Oxford: Clarendon Press, 1972), chap. 10. Jerry A. Fodor and Charles Chihara, 'Operationalism and Ordinary Language: A Critique of Wittgenstein,' in *Wittgenstein: The Philosophical Investigations*, ed. George Pitcher (Notre Dame, IN: University of Notre Dame Press, 1968).

16. Wittgenstein, *The Blue and Brown Books*, p. 51.

17. Benveniste, 'Subjectivity in Language,' in *Problems in General Linguistics*, pp. 223-231.

18. Christian Metz, 'The Imaginary Signifier,' in *The Imaginary Signifier: Psychoanalysis and the Cinema*, trans. Celia Britton *et al.* (Bloomington, IN: Indiana University Press, 1982), especially pp. 45-56. In formulating the concept of primary cinematic identification, Metz draws heavily on the work of Jean-Louis Baudry. See Baudry's 'Ideological Effects of the Basic Cinematographic Apparatus,' trans. Alan Williams, *Film Quarterly*, no. 28 (1974–1975), pp. 39-47; and 'The Apparatus,' trans. Jean Andrews and Bertrand Augst, *Camera Obscura*, no. 1 (1976), pp. 104-126. Both are reprinted in *Apparatus*, ed. Theresa Hak Kyung Cha (New York: Tanam Press, 1980).

The Avant-Garde:
Power, Change, and the Power to Change

Peter Lehman

During the last decade, a strong case has been made for the political and
ideological importance of avant-garde film. Stephen Heath's and Peter
Gidal's work on structural/materialist film exemplifies the best of this type
of theory and criticism. Their work goes hand in hand with ideological
critiques of dominant, narrative cinema. In the Winter 1976/77 issue of
Screen, Ben Brewster acknowledged, 'Gidal is right to emphasize the low
level of theorization of other kinds of film than narrative, and his criticisms
of *Screen*'s neglect in this respect are quite justified. . . .'[1] Accordingly, more
writing on experimental film was published in the latter years of the decade.
Both of these developments took place within the growing effort to ground
film theory within a truly Marxist-materialist philosophy. Thus, a central
figure like Heath not only has contributed significantly to both the ideological
critique of dominant, narrative cinema and the vigorous defense of
structural/materialist films, but also has published major articles on the
philosophy of materialism. By the end of the decade books such as Rosalind
Coward and John Ellis' *Language and Materialism* appeared.[2] The arguments
for the ideological importance of avant-garde texts are now inseparably
intertwined with the argument against idealism and for materialism.

During *The Revenge of the Pink Panther*, Inspector Clouseau and a
companion rush into an apartment in an attempt to escape their pursuers. As
luck would have it, it just happens to be Chief Inspector Dreyfus' apartment.
He awakes, overhears their conversation, and faints. His unconscious body
rolls out of bed and lies on the floor. Clouseau rushes over, rests Dreyfus' head
in his lap, and yells into his ear: 'Are you in there, former Chief Inspector
Dreyfus?' When there is no answer, he drops on the floor the seemingly

lifeless head, which lands with a thud. Most of us, no doubt, now have a more sophisticated notion of consciousness than Inspector Clouseau. We are less likely to posit some idealist essence 'in there'—before, outside of, above material historical process. I would argue, however, that a different and dangerous idealism has been implanted in the midst of the current argument for much of avant-garde film in general and structural/materialist film in particular.

Before attempting to outline that idealism and to suggest the complexities surrounding the problem, I want to make it clear that Heath's and Gidal's work on structural/materialist films seems to me essentially correct at the level at which they carry it out. I am also aware of the differences in their positions and am grouping them together only insofar as their work represents a common direction.[3] What, then, characterizes the problem?

Gidal and Heath frequently write as if the very style (and it is a style, contrary to what they imply) of structural/materialist films guarantees a spectatorial effect. Consider the following remarks from Gidal's 'Theory and Definition of Structural/Materialist Film':

> Through the usage of specific filmic devices such as repetition within duration one is *forced* to attempt to decipher the precise transformations that each co/incide/nce of cinematic techniques produces. . . . A materialist reading at one with the inscription of the work (which *is* the work) is enabled or *forced*. . . .[4] (emphasis mine)

And in an essay on Michael Snow's *Back and Forth*, Gidal similarly writes:

> We are *forced*, through the quickening pans, to *actively work* mentally to recapture the specifics of the defined space as we originally saw it. . . . We are totally aware of the relativism *forced* upon our senses through the specifically clearly defined (filmmaker's) actions with the camera.[5] (emphasis mine)

In these brief examples, the key word, to which I will return, is 'forced.' Another related set of terms that comes up frequently in writings on structural/materialist films is 'necessity' and 'demands.' Again from 'Theory and Definition of Structural/Materialist Film': 'The real time element *demands* such a consciousness and will.' And later:

> This attempt at verbalization, loose as it is, in fact is stating theoretically, beneath the surface, an aesthetic *necessitating* dialectic attempts at image arrestation, the *necessity* for production rather than consumption.[6] (emphasis mine)

Hand in hand with this *force* which necessitates and demands certain things, we find Gidal describing the process of watching structural/materialist films as one which can be charted with no qualifications. He tells us how the viewer is responding:

> Thus viewing such a film *is* at once viewing a film, and viewing the 'coming into presence' of the film, i.e., the system of consciousness that produces the work, that is produced by and in it. . . . The viewer *is* forming an equal and possibly more or less opposite 'film' in her/his head, constantly anticipating, correcting, recorrecting—constantly intervening in the arena of confrontation with the given reality, i.e., the isolated chosen area of each film's work, of each film's production.[7] (emphasis mine)

Gidal does not even qualify the process by writing that the viewer *may be* 'viewing' and 'forming' etc.; he writes with the certainty that the viewer *is*. Even such a qualification would be hopelessly inadequate in this context, since it begs the important question of which viewer under what circumstances *may* view the film in a certain way. In summary, then, Gidal's description of structural/materialist film posits a force which necessitates a response.

Despite differences in approach and object, consider Stephen Heath on Oshima's *In the Realm of the Senses*:

> Reactions and commentaries so far have made it only symptomatically clear that the *force* of *In the Realm of the Senses* . . . is that of a question decisively posed to cinema (and thus to *any* 'new' European or American cinema); a film which today remains untouched by that *force* will not be contemporary but ideologically reactionary.[8] (emphasis mine)

The use of the word 'force' here is not without interest, but what I wish to point to is the extraordinary emphasis on a linear advance. Any film which follows in the wake of *In the Realm of the Senses* but ignores it is a reactionary film. Thus the model posits a linear, progressive, art historical movement. In a parallel way Gidal refers several times to 'retrograde' work, e.g., 'Magritte's retrograde picture-puzzle-gimmicks.'[9] We are told about 'advanced filmmakers' and about work which performs 'rearguard revision.' Implicit in this notion of the advance guard is the rear guard. Developments are seen as successive and interrelated. But how accurate is this configuration, which reminds one of Susan Sontag's complaint that the term avant-garde connotes columns of marching artists, some few in the lead with the others following?[10] But is anyone in fact leading and is anyone following? Poor Oshima himself must be confusedly running back and forth since *Empire of Passion*, the film which in fact did succeed *In the Realm of the Senses*, looks in many ways like a film which has ignored the 'force' of his own previous film.

I suggest that much contemporary criticism of avant-garde film has falsely emphasized the power and force of avant-garde styles, and that this problem stems from a failure to understand the status of a style in the complex of styles which characterize the pluralism of advanced capitalist, technological society.[11] In other words, a new style today is not what a new style was two hundred years ago.

Some of the most important art historical criticism of our time has focused on the viewer's interaction with the visual image. E.H. Gombrich devotes a great deal of attention in *Art and Illusion* to what he calls 'the beholder's share,' and Michael Baxandall details what he calls the 'cognitive style' in *Painting and Experience in Fifteenth Century Italy*.[12] The modern viewer looks at 15th-century paintings and sees different things than did the contemporaneous viewer. Relatedly, there were class differences among producers, owners and viewers of art in 15th-century Italy, only some of whom, for example, were trained to deal with paintings in relationship to geometry and mathematics. As time passed, some of these skills used by the 15th-century viewers were lost. As Baxandall so well states:

> We have been moving toward a notion of a Quattrocento cognitive style. By this one would mean the equipment that the 15th-century painter's public brought to complex visual stimulations like pictures. One is talking not about all 15th-century people, but about those whose response to works of art was important to the artist—the patronizing classes, one might say. In effect this means rather a small proportion of the population: mercantile and professional men, acting as members of confraternities or as individuals, princes and their courtiers, the senior members of religious houses. The peasants and the urban poor play a very small part in the Renaissance culture that most interests us now, which may be deplorable but is a fact that must be accepted. Yet among the patronizing classes there were variations, not just the inevitable variation from man to man, but variations by groups.[13]

Certain people in 15th-century Italy, for example, developed the mathematical and geometrical skills referred to earlier because of economics, the marketplace and their specific class. Their skills were brought to bear by them when they looked at paintings. At one point, Baxandall succinctly writes: 'Uccello's pictorial style must meet the proper cognitive style for the picture to work.'[14] It is this notion of a historical, culturally determined cognitive style which is lacking in Gidal's and Heath's work. Thus, they pay absolutely no attention whatsoever to what we would call the cognitive style of the 1970s and 80s viewer of avant-garde films. They posit a general viewer and thus avoid asking a series of questions: What part of the total population watches these films? What is the relationship of different strata of the audience to the artists who produce the films? What particular skills do these people bring to the viewing process? What functions do the films fulfill for these viewers? What are the relationships between the skills the viewer brings, the functions the work has for the viewer, and his/her economic class and educational background? Neither Peter Gidal in 'Theory and Definition of Structural/Materialist Film' nor Stephen Heath in 'Repetition Time: Notes Around Structural/Materialist Films' hint at anything related to such questions.[15] For work done on the avant-garde in the name of Marxist-materialism, this is particularly curious and relates also, I think, to the second major problem in this kind of work.

Pluralism is one of the central facts of the dominant contemporary cognitive style. Currently, work in all the arts goes on in several different directions simultaneously: various forms of abstract painting and representational painting; twelve-tone, electronic, and traditional harmonic music; narrative films and structural/materialist films, etc. This has not always been the case in Western art. The dominance of a single style in a given time period and the attendant notion of the succession of stylistic movement was once a more accurate description of the arts than it is now. This change has led Leonard Meyer to claim: 'If the Renaissance is over, then the avant-garde is ended.'[16] Is it possible that the real question is not whether the avant-garde possesses the force and power which Gidal and Heath attribute to it, but whether the avant-garde exists? Is it possible that the categorical conception 'avant-garde' makes us see a false set of interrelationships among diverse styles? Is there currently an 'advanced' style? If so, to where is it advancing? And is there a 'rear' style stumbling along behind or threatening to hold back the advanced style?

The pluralism that defines the contemporary moment in the arts cannot be separated from the function of art in our culture—and that function, of course, cannot be separated from economics. The image is created for sale in our culture; it is pried loose from any immediately practical context and given an aesthetic context which in turn is intricately related to its value as a commodity. Jackson Pollock's paintings occupy the same space both literally and functionally as Constable's paintings: literally in the sense that one can see paintings by both artists in the same museums; functionally, in the sense that they are to be briefly contemplated before one moves on to the next image. Of course, the rich can buy them, take them home, and hang them on their walls for more sustained contemplation. The Pollock is valued for the individual hand of the artist just as much as the Constable. Even Andy Warhol's attempts at making fun of this notion of art are valued because they are *Warhol's* attempts. We have had since the early part of this century a revolution in the styles of art, but not in its function—we have had half a revolution. In this case, half a revolution may be worse than no revolution at all, since it has fooled us. Styles simply do not, in and of themselves, have the force to effect what we want of them.

Several people have recently addressed this crucial area. Paul Willemen, responding to John Ellis' argument concerning the radical potential supplied by pornography's shifting regimes of representation, notes: 'If women are to conduct this struggle on their own, this is likely to lead to nothing but a change in the forms of porn, not in its function.'[17] Though his terms are slightly different ('forms' instead of 'styles'), he quite rightly emphasizes that it is dangerous to overestimate shifts in pornographic representations without considering the functions of those shifting styles. Writing about Susan Sontag's work on photography, John Berger observes:

> The theory of the current use of photographs leads me to ask whether photography might serve a different function. Is there an alternative photographic practice? The question should not be answered naively. Today no alternative professional practice (if one thinks of the profession of photographer) is possible. The system can accomodate any photograph.[18]

Heath and Gidal have not been entirely silent upon these issues. In his article 'Difference,' Heath argues that the spectator addressed by a film is not the same thing as any given spectating individual: each spectator has a unique and complex social and psychoanalytic history which determines individual response. Heath gives as an example his memory of a personal response while watching *The Collector*: he recognizes a street which he has seen, thinks about other Wyler films, and gets caught up in an obsession involving eggs, the color yellow and the name Eggar.[19] Obviously this precise response is located at the level of the uniquely individual and cannot be controlled by a style or anything else. Indeed, no one has ever argued that any style can control or determine response at this level.

In an article entitled 'Context,' which appears at the end of a collection of essays, *Questions of Cinema*, Heath returns to this problem. The arguments concerning a film's 'real effect,' he points out, frequently end up by polarizing the viewer-text relationship:

> Debate around films often stumbles over issues of effectivity, 'the real effect of a film,' deadlocks on either 'the text itself,' its meaning 'in it,' or else the text as non-existent other than 'outside itself,' in the particular responses it happens to engage from any individual or individual audience—the text 'closed' or 'open.' The reading (viewing, reception, understanding, reaction) of a film, however, must be seen as neither constrained absolutely nor free absolutely but historical, and that historically includes the determinations of the institution of cinema, the conditions of the production of meanings, of specific terms of address (or engagement of reading).[20]

If there is a problem with this formulation, it is only that Heath does not develop his own insight. The passage is the only one of its kind in a book which raises many profound questions about cinema, but none of the specific historical, economic ones which would help us construct the cognitive style that the successful viewer of structural/materialist films brings to his/her viewing. Nor are any specific questions posed about who that viewer is. Though 'Repetition Time' is reprinted, nothing in the volume disturbs the generalized account of those films, an account which seems to describe all spectators and no spectators.

Gidal's comments in this area are briefer than Heath's, although very revealing. He cautions: 'Form must be distinguished from style, otherwise it serves merely in its reactionary sense to mean formalism. . . .'[21] And in a curious footnote he writes, 'Actual *power* over the cinema-goer none of us has at this stage.'[22] The first quotation testifies to Gidal's desire that structural/ materialist film be not merely another style. 'Form is meant as formal operation, not as composition.'[23] But this bypasses the crucial question as to how the spectator will have access to this 'operation.'

A symptomatic contradiction seems evident to me in Gidal's harsh criticism of certain reviews of his films. For example, Gidal's attack on Lucy Fischer and Jonas Mekas for diversionary readings of his works indicates less a failure of theirs than a failure of his formulations.[24] The cognitive styles of Fischer and Mekas surely include film-viewing skills lacking in the great majority of the population; yet Gidal can find horrible failures in their readings. How can Gidal posit a force and a power within his films defined in terms of spectator effect when those effects do not match what even learned, specialized spectators report? Supposedly the films have a force and power that demand a particular response, but these viewers do not acquiesce. Instead of criticizing the viewers for failing his films' demands, perhaps Gidal should reconsider his own conception of the films' demands. And how, after all this, can a professed Marxist materialist simply state in a footnote that all the power he has been speaking of is not actual anyway?

I have had private discussions with both Heath and Gidal concerning my objections to their positions on avant-garde art. Interestingly, they both used the word 'pessimistic' in response. It seems to them unlikely that anything will change, but they see the danger of landing in a position which seems to point towards the uselessness of attempts at transformation. Now, the position that I am trying to argue is precisely that things are not hopeless. What leads to hopelessness and pessimism is placing such emphasis on the power of avant-garde movements.

Heath and Gidal have been very important in showing the tenacity that idealism holds over Western culture. But can a Marxist-materialist, interventionist position be built upon an argument of such theoretical purity that it cuts itself off from any need to actually weigh the impact of structural/ materialist films upon actual audiences who live in history, in economics, in culture? If the project of overthrowing idealism (often allied to overthrowing mere academicism) leads us to conclude that change is unlikely, then it is necessary that we recast the problem in other terms. What, briefly, are those terms and in what new direction could further work on the avant-garde move?

At one of the simplest levels, Steve Neale has recently pointed to the need to do more work on conditions of exhibition. Regarding showing avant-garde films in auditoriums designed for traditional cinema he writes: 'Alienation and anxiety become amplified, however, when the films are viewed in conditions designed solely for identification and spectacle.'[25] He is obviously right, and yet much of the work I have been referring to on avant-garde bypasses or minimizes even this simple concern with the actual historical and cultural circumstances of projection. Heath and Gidal write about structural/materialist films as if the kind of theater in which we view them were of minor importance. Yet the so-called force of the film is obviously in part the force of the conditions of projection.

But this is only a simple beginning; the issues are much more complex. What if we did redesign the auditorium? What if, at times, we even took out the seats and asked the viewers to move around the room during projection or turned light bulbs off and on during the screenings? Obviously, it would have some effect on the way in which the audience reacted to the film. But not as much as one might at first presume.

The function that art has in our culture and the institutionalization of that function work strongly to contain anything which seems radical. If one is in the habit of going to the movies once a week and spending an hour and a half in the dark and then one week *In the Realm of the Senses* is there but the next week *California Suite* is showing, that context is not negligible. The same holds true for those few in our culture who attend avant-garde screenings at art museums or film societies. The unexpected, for example, can easily come to be expected, and the museum theater can be just as comforting as the Majestic. The image is still for sale and it still occupies that special space which has dominated Western art for so long—the aesthetic space. It is, when all is said and done, just one style seen in the same space where last week a diffcrent style was seen and next week yet another style can be seen.

The power of the institutionalization of the image within our culture is clear with reference to the simple experience of walking through the rooms of an art museum. Most people who visit art museums can calmly walk between two rooms, one of which contains Pollock paintings and the other of which contains Constable paintings. This sharply pluralistic aesthetic experience is part of a currently widespread cognitive style. The way we look at anything in any room in any art museum or at anything projected on any screen in any theater is profoundly shaped, qualified and conditioned by this simple fact.

In a discussion of the processes of spectatorship Jean-François Lyotard has compared the position of the viewer of a non-abstract painting to that of a client, and the position of the viewer of a Pollock painting to that of a victim.[26] We might then expect the experience of the modern museum to be that of being a client in the fifth room one walks through, a victim in the sixth, and a client in the seventh. But the continuity of seeing various images in deeply similar ways from room to room in fact militates against such a yo-yo effect. If Lyotard's description were not lacking in some fundamental way, the National Gallery made a serious mistake when it opened its new wing with, among other things, a room devoted to Pollock. Lyotard makes Pollock sound like much more of a threat to the powers that be in Washington, D.C. than John Hinckley.

In fact it doesn't matter if there is no framed, easel art in the room or if there are no chairs in the theater—all of these experiences have a profound aesthetic continuity. Any reading of a film's or a painting's 'force' which does not address this is drastically over-simplifying. The continuities supplied by the museums and theaters are more basic than the supposedly drastically different effects produced by the styles contained therein. From this perspective, everything contained in those rooms is just another style—the function remains the same. Everything in those rooms is both literally and ideologically contained. This would indicate that we need to make lesser claims for the force of styles such as those of structural/materialist films and stronger claims for the force of, say, the Museum of Modern Art.

In 'Power and Photography,' John Tagg observes:

> In the domain of photography what this implies is not an attempt to devise a single stylistic strategy which will meet all contingencies, but a determination to begin the work of mapping out certain positions within an indeterminate field. We must pinpoint those strategic kinds of interaction which both open up different social arenas of action and sketch the institutional order of the practice by deploying or developing new modes of production, distribution, circulation; by exploiting different formats; by evolving different formal solutions; by cutting different trajectories across the ruling codes of pictorial meaning; and by establishing different relationships both with those who are pictured and those who view the pictures. There is no center to such a strategy; only a multiplicity of local incursions in a constantly shifting ground of tactical actions—specific contexts which link up with others in all sorts of ways, which may hold significance for a chain of related struggles, and which are the precondition for any more concerted confrontation.[27]

This is precisely what we need to do for film. To achieve this, it is necessary to discard certain notions about the nature of the avant-garde's importance. The search for one, true 'advanced' style of filmmaking—say, that of Gidal—even one key film—say, *In the Realm of the Senses*—as a universal ideological standard against which other styles and films are measured is, finally, a gravely defective project. We must qualify what we mean when we say a film occupies an advance-guard *or* rearguard position, taking into account a variety of social circumstances. For much of our population who do not have the cognitive style to watch a structural/ materialist film, it is more retrograde for them to do so and daydream, fall asleep, or walk out than to watch a Hollywood film in a knowledge-producing context (e.g., analytical, ideological discussion—preceding, following, or even during projection). I am neither for a reactionary swing away from the avant-garde to Hollywood, nor for a mindless pluralism, which innocently views styles as free from ideologies. But it is necessary to engage the problem of specificity of circumstances within which any film is consumed. And this requires that we accord certain elements of the avant-garde a less central position and stop arrogantly dismissing other elements of the avant-garde (e.g., Gidal on 'New American Cinema'),[28] let alone Hollywood.

Today a small, educated, financially comfortable group of people has the cognitive style needed to properly watch avant-garde films, and, predictably, the rest of the population lacks this skill. Thus, as during the Renaissance, there is a close relationship between the producers and the viewers who share the necessary cognitive style. The same small group of people who knowledgeably watch these films writes the letters of support that help get the grants for the people who make them. In some cases, the committees who grant the awards are comprised of the people who share this cognitive style. There is, indirectly, a patronizing class as there was during the Renaissance. Interestingly, the money is usually just enough to complete the film and keep the filmmaker struggling along, but never enough to make a broad distribution conceivable. Thus, the filmmaker remains dependent on the praise, support and recognition of a limited number of people to continue his/her work. This specific economic structure (one of many that need more detailed study) actually helps guarantee that no large audience is ever required for the avant-garde filmmaker to keep working. In fact, one can safely conclude that the one thing avant-garde filmmakers never need and never have is a large audience. But the audience they have is exactly the one they need to keep working without expanding their audience. 'The peasants and the urban poor play a very small part in the Renaissance culture that most interests us now, which may be deplorable but is a fact that must be accepted.'[29] Unless we effectively recast the problem of force and power, that is precisely the way future film historians will end up characterizing structural/materialist films.

NOTES

1. Ben Brewster, 'Afterword,' in *Structural Film Anthology*, ed. Peter Gidal (London: British Film Institute, 1978), p. 144.

2. Rosalind Coward and John Ellis, *Language and Materialism* (London: Routledge & Kegan Paul, 1977).

3. For an indication of the differences between them, see Peter Gidal's letter in 'Point of View,' *Wide Angle*, vol. 2, no. 4 (1978), p. 86, and Stephen Heath's reply in 'Point of View,' *Wide Angle*, vol. 3, no. 2 (1979), p. 79.

4. Peter Gidal, 'Theory and Definition of Structural/Materialist Film,' in *Structural Film Anthology*, pp. 1, 7.

5. Gidal, 'Back and Forth,' in *Structural Film Anthology*, p. 46.

6. Gidal, 'Theory and Definition,' pp. 9, 17.

7. Ibid., pp. 2, 3.

8. Stephen Heath, 'The Question Oshima,' *Wide Angle*, vol. 2, no. 1 (1977), p. 48.

9. Gidal, 'Theory and Definition,' p. 12.

10. In an interview with Dick Cavett on PBS. The militaristic connotations of the term avant-garde are interesting in relation to the use of such power-oriented words as 'force' and 'demand.'

11. See also Malcolm Le Grice, *Abstract Film and Beyond* (London: Studio Vista, 1977). Many of the points I make about Gidal and Heath have exact parallels in Le Grice's work. See the use of the words 'forces' (p. 139), 'demand' (pp. 139, 140), 'advance' (pp. 120, 152) and 'reactionary' (p. 153). Le Grice also describes a process which he assumes takes place in a generalized viewer watching a particular film (p. 120), and uses the word 'must' in a related way (p. 140). Le Grice also claims that features of the films he praises are at times more than a style: 'This is not just a question of style, but more fundamental.' (p. 88.) Le Grice's conclusion presents a progressive view of film history in general (pp. 152-53).

12. E.H. Gombrich, *Art and Illusion* (Princeton, NJ: Princeton University Press, 1961), and Michael Baxandall, *Painting and Experience in Fifteenth Century Italy* (London: Oxford University Press, 1976).

13. Baxandall, pp. 38–39.

14. Ibid., p. 91.

15. Stephen Heath, 'Repetition Time: Notes Around "Structural/Materialist Films," ' *Wide Angle*, vol. 2, no. 3 (1978), pp. 4–11.

16. Leonard Meyer, *Music, the Arts, and Ideas* (Chicago, IL: University of Chicago Press, 1976),

p. 169. I am here recapitulating some points I have argued at greater length elsewhere. See my 'Style, Function and Ideology: A Problem in Film History,' *Film Reader*, no. 4 (1979), pp. 73–80.

17. Paul Willemen, 'Letter to John,' *Screen*, vol. 21, no. 2 (1980), p. 64.

18. John Berger, *About Looking* (New York: Pantheon Books, 1980), p. 56.

19. Stephen Heath, 'Difference,' *Screen*, vol. 19, no. 3 (1978), p. 107.

20. Stephen Heath, *Questions of Cinema* (London: Macmillan & Co., 1981), pp. 242–243.

21. Gidal, 'Theory and Definition,' p. 2.

22. Ibid., p. 21.

23. Ibid., p. 2.

24. Ibid., pp. 17–18.

25. Steve Neale, 'Oppositional Exhibition: Notes and Problems,' *Screen*, vol. 21, no. 3 (1980–1981), p. 54.

26. Jean-François Lyotard, 'Acinema,' *Wide Angle*, vol. 2, no. 3 (1978), pp. 57–59.

27. John Tagg, 'Power and Photography: Part One,' *Screen Education*, no. 26 (1980), p 49.

28. Gidal, 'Theory and Definitions,' p. 13.

29. Baxandall, pp. 38–39.

The Retraction of State Funding of Film and Video Arts and Its Effects on Future Practice

Maureen Turim

Under the aegis of the Reagan administration, the National Endowment for the Arts revised its 'Application Guidelines for 1982.' Reagan's changes were made so late that the guidelines booklet was published as a curious document, its original program covered with obliterating marks and supplemented by errata sheets. The past history of the NEA had been literally rubber-stamped 'INVALID.'

The marks of erasure disclose proposed cuts in Federal funding of 50%, from $176.6 million to $88.4 million.[1] These cuts are distributed differently to various programs; this differential turns out to be an ideological strategy of regulation so pervasive that one wonders how the statement of 'Goals and Basic Policy' by the National Council of the NEA escaped such graphic censorship. We still read the following proclamation:

> It is not the intention of this statement to define 'art.' The term is to be understood in its broadest sense; that is, with full cognizance of the pluralistic nature of the arts in America, with a deliberate decision to disclaim any endorsement of an 'official' art and with a full commitment to artistic freedom.[2]

And we still find a goal labeled 'Making the Arts Available' that promises:

> To insure that all Americans have a true opportunity to make an informed, an educated choice to have the arts of high quality touch their lives so that no person is deprived access to the arts by reason of:
> —Geography
> —Inadequate Income
> —Inadequate Education

—Physical or Mental Handicaps
—Social or cultural patterns unresponsive to diverse ethnic group
needs.[3]

Though no marks of erasure appear over these words, it is obvious from the programmatic changes made in the NEA that, in fact, 1982 marks an attempt to substantially redefine the art and culture of this country. This paper will attempt to trace the history under erasure, and discuss the means of resistance to these authoritarian strategies of capital.

In 1969 Francis O'Connor published *Public Funding for the Arts; the WPA and Now,* positioning his discussion as an appeal to the still nascent National Endowment for the Arts and Humanities. He builds his argument toward a series of organizational recommendations aimed at setting policies for the 1970s. O'Connor argues for the development of a type of funding that would be radically different from that of the 1930s, the type of funding that comes close to the kinds of principles the NEA/NEH were beginning to implement before the Reagan budget cuts.[4]

I will briefly assess the experience of public funding in the 1930s, drawing on O'Connor's research. But I will supplement his account with an ideological analysis of 1930s art, focusing on developments in painting and the graphic arts. Then I will try to indicate how this experience was transformed in the reemergence of government funding in the middle of the 1960s and its considerable expansion in the 1970s.

Government funding of the arts in this country began, as is well known, in 1933, when Roosevelt formed the Public Works of Art Project (PWAP). The PWAP was designed as a short-term emergency measure (December, 1933 to June 30, 1934) aimed at helping some of the 10,000 unemployed artists. In fact, O'Connor's description of the PWAP invites an analysis of a restrained program of investment in cheap artistic labor. Artists were hired by the government to decorate public buildings with emblems of liberal democratic ideology. After the program ended, five months passed without any government funding. Then mural production was reorganized under the 'Section on Painting and Sculpture' of the Treasury Department. The official instructions asked that the murals it commissioned illustrate the 'American Scene.' While an implied conservatism of subject matter and representational form favored the regionalists, this policy subsequently nurtured a sort of capitalist realism, etching post offices and courthouses with an ideal vision of a melting-pot populace fervently retooling industry through a beneficent technology, a dream of bountiful harvests, efficient communication and fair and valid justice. Monumentality was traced with mythological reference and Greek revival to ennoble the ordinary and depict a utopian fantasy of harmonious socioeconomic functioning.

The WPA Federal Arts Project did tend to achieve more autonomy and diversity than the Section on Painting and Sculpture. Begun in 1935, the WPA funded the production of innovative mural projects, painting, printmaking, rural and community arts workshops, and research projects such as the famous Index of American Design. Some of this was still linked to the Treasury Department, which provided commissioned WPA works to be hung in government buildings. However, the project structure of the WPA—grants to individual artists, equipment development grants (as in the case of lithography and seriography) and outreach service programs—anticipates the granting structure of the NEA.

In 1941 the Roosevelt administration started cutting off government funds to the arts through both programs as part of a policy of highest priority for increased military spending and the 'support the war' effort. The few artists who did receive government paychecks during the war did so directly through a branch of the armed forces. Although some money was made available for a while longer, the Federal Arts Project had, in effect, lasted from 1935 to 1940.

During these years some aspects of what might be properly called *public funding* had indeed occurred; monies were allocated to artists for the experimental and exploratory development of culture. However, this gesture should be seen in historical context. O'Connor discusses how basic conceptions of the program always fluctuated between economic relief to needy artists and a patronage system in which the quality of the product was of central importance. But it is also germane to stress an ideological split between an art functioning as *use-value* in the recuperation of an ailing capitalism and an art that defines itself as strategically apart from an emblematic federalism and corporate imperatives.

The artists had a militant, organized union that actively protested cuts and decisions to which they objected. Even so, many artists felt government funding could serve to ameliorate the potential threat of art as a subversive tactic. In the struggle between Roosevelt and labor, *The New Masses* provided artists of the 1930s with a vital alternative to the WPA. Lithography and seriography were used as popular, subversive media; the unionized artists were drawn to such projects as commemorating the assassinations of striking steelworkers. As we shall see in the discussion of the development of the National Endowments that follows, government funding can appear to undercut dissent. However, its effect cannot be reduced to a simple appropriation of artistic expression and co-optation of dissident voices and images, given the very different context that has evolved.

Between 1943 and 1965 there was *no* program of federal funding of the arts. How should we explain the reinstitution of governmental funding? More than one factor can be invoked. One explanation is the entrance of liberals into national administrations in the 1960s. They had available a prototype, the New York State Council on the Arts, established by Nelson Rockefeller in 1960. The history of the NYSCA runs parallel to that of the National Endowments, but preceded its development by five years. The NYSCA can be seen as having served as a kind of model for the NEA at various stages. In the first few years of operation, the NYSCA concentrated on the traditional high arts, but included what were termed 'ghetto projects,' which actively sought minority applicants. The social strategy of such a program was to ease the 'crisis in the cities' on two fronts: by encouraging an urban renaissance among the middle and upper classes; and by easing racial and class tensions among the poor through cultural community involvement. On a national level such policies could provide an 'aesthetic environment' for sunbelt industries and be part of an attempt to calm Detroit, Milwaukee, Watts and Newark. But as easy as it is to read such funding as a sociopolitical strategy of containment, it is also too simple to dismiss it as that—for the energies awakened by such activity are not necessarily subject to control simply because the source of their funding is governmental. This is an issue to which I will return at the conclusion of the paper.

Another factor in the reinstitution of federal funding was the gradual acceptance, towards the late 1950s, of innovative American Abstraction as an emblem of 'American freedom,' in contrast to the Soviet repression of artists under the doctrine of Socialist Realism. The U.S. could literally afford to trade in a 19th-century monumental heritage for a new social sign, American avant-garde. It was always somewhat grating to read the annual reports of the NEA or NYSCA, or to have to write a grant to conform to their institutional expectations. All artistic expression had to be recuperated as national identity or civic pride, with the subtext of this being, ultimately, good economic investment. (Kitty Carlisle, head of the NYSCA said, 'The arts are good for business,' and proceeded to quote tourism revenue statistics for New York City.)[5] Thus funding and reception began to fill in the ambiguous artistic signs of abstraction.

Even so, the policy the NEA adopted in the 1970s was one of unconditional funding of innovative projects by unknown artists who lacked commercial acceptance. This was essentially the policy O'Connor suggested in his 1969 study. It is true that the greatest percentage of funding was allocated to institutions rather than individuals, and for traditional conservative endeavors (museums, symphonies, operas and ballets) rather than experimentation. But, over the last few years, there have been increasing efforts to include within certain funding categories the photographer, the craftsperson, the avant-garde artist and the leftist. It is precisely these areas of funding that have been hit hardest by the revision of the guidelines in response to the Reagan cutbacks.

Consider the important category called Visual Arts Fellowships, which for 1982 covered visual artists working in all media. In the original document written before the cutbacks, the statement reads, 'Visual Artists of exceptional talent and demonstrated ability of any aesthetic persuasion' can apply, and 'fellowship awards are based primarily on the quality of an artist's work as demonstrated by the visual material submitted in the application.' The revised message states that funding will be considered only for '*practicing professional artists* of exceptional talent and demonstrated ability,' and the review criteria have been changed to include, in addition to the quality of work submitted, a record of professional activity and achievement, and evidence that the applicant's work reflects continued, serious and exceptional aesthetic investigation. There are also the following encouraging words:

> In recent years only 3% of fellowship applications have been funded; competition continues to increase. There is nothing to be gained by submitting work, unless it is ready to be evaluated in a rigorous professional context.[6]

By the late 1970s the NEA and media grant section of NEH (founded in 1972) had created grants for film and video art as well as documentary expression, and had adopted relatively loose structures. As a result, they were funding projects and film and video makers of interest. In 1980 the *Cultural Post*, the house journal of the Endowments, could publish an article promoting roles played by the NEH media grants in producing such left-leaning documentaries as *The Wobblies*, *Harlan County*, etc. But the gesture of institutional pride in the progressive directions its funding was taking to produce quality social documentation is now entirely a historical curiosity. Consider the attitude of Richard Bishirjian, the head of the Reagan transitional team to investigate the NEH, as presented in *Newsweek*:

> Bishirjian found that the endowment was 'inundated with junk'—a charge he backed up by singling out a $753,000 grant to make a film about textile workers in North Carolina. Bishirjian approved, however, of a smaller grant for a film about Carl Sandburg. 'The life of Carl Sandburg touches millions. I'm not interested in the lives of workers.'[7]

The cuts in NEA and NEH funding rationalized by this kind of attitude are having a wide range of effects. The NEH media grants were often made for documentaries that were shown on PBS, so the cuts to this program will have important debilitating effects on the information available to the American public. As Jim Hoberman has pointed out, NEH media grants were cut more severely than NEA (from $9.5 million to $3.8 million).[8] But in assessing the cuts to individual film and video artists, we must remember that the funding of individuals was always the weakest part of the NEA program. Whereas documentary projects were funded by the NEH as well as by NEA production grants and fellowships, the individual video artist was eligible for direct funding only through the NEH Fellowship program and the filmmaker only through AFI filmmakers' grants. At the height of funding in the late 1970s, the grants were always under $12,000 per year and were by definition non-renewable. Not only were the fellowships made biennial in 1981, but also they are now the only source of funding available to photographers and craftspeople, previously funded in separate categories. The AFI distributes a total of $400,000 in filmmakers grants. Thus we must realize that the categories of grants, the distribution of funds, and the amounts available for film and video work were always frustratingly inadequate and only minimally responsive to the living needs of individual artists.

The NEA was far more important to avant-garde film and video than it would appear from the above remarks. This is due to the funding made in two categories: Major Media Centers and Services to the Field. For although individuals only received money indirectly from these granting categories, the institutions thus funded were the major developers of equipment, the providers of equipment access and training, and the forums for distribution, exhibition, discussion and criticism of avant-garde and independent works.

If one takes just the case of New York City, the impact of these grants becomes clear. The Anthology Film Archives, Millennium, the Collective for Living Cinema, Film Forum, The Kitchen (Center for Video and Dance), Global Village, Cable Arts Foundation, Cable Soho and the exhibition programs at the Museum of Modern Art and the Whitney Museum of American Art all received grants from at least one of these categories. These institutions have helped make experimental film and television viable cultural forces. NYSCA's role in funding arts institutions helps explain why so many institutions are found in New York City, for these institutions were dependent on receiving state and national funding. By supporting such institutions nationally, granting agencies sustained creative filmmaking in this country. If these institutions and parallel facilities in Chicago, Berkeley, Philadelphia, Los Angeles, Houston, Minneapolis, etc. go under, there will be *no* alternative film and video.

Equipment development and access facilities receive grants under the Services to the Field category. These institutions provide young artists with tools and facilities. Particularly in the case of experimental video, such shared, publicly funded facilities are crucial. Commercial production fees are not only exorbitant for the independent artist, but commercial production houses have a different attitude towards equipment design and use. The artist needs non-commercial facilities that offer an alternative to a mainstream 'special effects' approach to image alteration. The few such alternative equipment facilities that exist are severely threatened by cuts in national funding. As is the case with the Major Media Centers grants and individual artists grants, some of the initial damage of national funding cuts may be buffered by stable funding from the individual state councils. One wonders not only how long such funding will remain available, but also about the logic of treating centers of national importance as if they were the financial responsibility solely of the state in which they are located.

One of the justifications given by the Reagan administration for cutting government funding is the insistence that within capitalism 'private philanthropy,' not government aid, is the proper source of funding for art. This notion recalls the glory days of the Rockefellers and Carnegies, times that were riddled with contradictions between the rich maximizing profit and presenting a generous public presence through charity. In some senses this model is outdated; the contemporary corporation does not have the same ideological incentives for contributions to the arts as did the robber barons of late 19th-century American capitalism. Tax incentives and advertising are the strongest motivations for corporate contributions to the arts, but these incentives are less likely to raise revenues for art than might at first be apparent, as the history of corporate donations has shown.

Corporations are elegible to deduct up to 5% of their net taxable income for charitable contributions. Despite this government subsidy for charity, many major corporations do not contribute at all, and few give over 2%.[9] Furthermore, because advertising is their other incentive, corporations seek to have their names associated with non-controversial art. The avant-garde does not have the internal apparatus to appeal for corporate funding, nor would its more daring works appeal to the largely conservative aesthetics of corporate decision-makers. As for the documentaries once funded by the liberal peer review committees of the NEH, commercial sponsorship has already proven hazardous—witness the withdrawal of Mobil support for one of the *Middletown* segments by Peter Davis broadcast on PBS in the spring of 1982.

The peer review structure of the NEH and the NEA had been used by certain corporations to determine which projects to assist, and that system is now in jeopardy. Peer autonomy is threatened by revised guidelines, increased directorial power in the hands of newly appointed conservatives, and by a Heritage Foundation report that blamed peer review for all of the ills of the National Endowments.[10] Even if corporations are interested in contributing to independent progressive arts organizations or individuals, they will find it difficult without such a selection process. As a result, large, traditional performing arts groups with full-time fundraisers on their staffs will probably receive whatever contributions corporations make. Thus, while it is true that corporations contributed three times as much as the National Endowments to arts projects even during the height of NEA/NEH funding, they never contributed much to the experimental and political sector of artistic production; and there is nothing in current policy that might encourage corporations to step into this funding breach.

Response to this crisis in arts funding presents a curious picture of U.S. attitudes about the arts and humanities. Few people seem to assess the value of funding art and culture as a vital force of creative and political expression in our society.

The disinterest comes from more than one quarter. First, there is the strong conservative, anti-intellectual streak that actively attacks contemporary aesthetic and intellectual activity. One of the purest expressions of this is a *Reader's Digest* article, 'While You're Up, Get Me a Grant!' The opening paragraph expresses the narrowmindedness of the attack in a series of rhetorical questions:

> Interested in 'The Romantic Poetry of the Young Karl Marx'? Or the 'Folk Rituals of Birth, Marriage and Death Among Urban Polish-Americans'? Or 'The Contribution of the Gay Experience to American Visual Arts'?[11]

For the right wing, these are 'dubious' projects. But the attack on both the National Endowments and U.S. artistic and intellectual activity comes from other positions as well, and can even be made by potential beneficiaries of government funding.

Some artists take a position critical of the NEA, its bureaucratic structure and the funding choices it made even in its more liberal phase. Filmmaker Bruce Connor is among those who have stated that the NEA 'should be done away with entirely.' His individualist position proposes that artists choose only creative projects within very limited means, like his own films.[12]

Some opponents of artistic abstraction believe the cuts will radicalize artists and end the formalist tendencies of U.S. art. This position fails to attribute any interpretive value to art which functions on a level of abstraction. It would cleanse artistic tendencies that are politically unacceptable through whatever means are necessary. Like the romantic individualist, the political polemicist is naive about contemporary culture in advanced capitalism.

Both the individualist artist and the polemicist need cultural circuits for distribution and exhibition of their works. It is hard to see how anyone can gain from the economic repression that will ensue after the dissolution of the liberal structures which have benefited the growth of arts that do not primarily generate profit. We also need to see that fertile cultural moments demand a tension between the formal and the referential. Radical spirit can be expressed in an abstract form, but too many are seeking only literal expressions of cultural resistance.

Finally, a certain inertia in responding to funding cuts for the arts grows out of the overwhelming anger and depression people feel concerning the simultaneous cuts in social programs. If poverty and unemployment are deemed necessary by a government to stop inflation and balance the budget, how can one muster protest about the cuts in funding intellectual research and aesthetic and cultural expression? Even social documentation seems less direct an issue than the suffering of people betrayed by their government.

However, this ignores the larger picture of government spending and financial planning, increased military budgets of the Reagan years, and tax benefits to the corporations and the wealthy. Other solutions are possible for the current economic crisis, solutions that would neither throw more Americans into desperate poverty nor cripple the arts and humanities. We are once again faced with the concealing of government spending on the military and the subsidizing of corporate profit while we are told there is no money for cultural, educational or health needs.

A way of understanding the connection between arts funding and welfare and social services programs that are being cut is to consider the Expansion Arts program of the NEA. The new chairman of the NEA, Frank Hodsoll, sees this program, which concentrates on ways to provide minorities with cultural expression, as being primarily 'educational.'[13] Once he labels it as such, he will be able to divorce this program from the redefined NEA goals. In conservative fashion, this ignores how economic deprivation and the history of racial oppression has robbed Black and Spanish people of their own artistic heritage. If this meager attempt at restoration of cultural diversity, of proud racial voices, is an educational goal, it is a lesson that the U.S. needs now more than ever. So rather than setting social services up in competition with cultural expression, we need to link them as our concerns.

NOTES

1. The statistics quoted on budget cuts are those announced at the time of the 'Cinema Histories, Cinema Practices' conference, and, although some monies have been restored, the basic situation described in the article remains the same.

2. National Endowment for the Arts, *Application Guidelines for 1982* (Washington, DC: G.P.O., 1982).

3. Ibid.

4. Francis O'Connor, *Public Funding for the Arts: the WPA and Now* (Greenwich, CT: New York Graphic Society, 1969).

5. This was the argument presented by Carlisle in numerous public addresses throughout the state, including a talk in Binghamton, New York in Spring of 1979. A more recent study by The Port of Authority of New York and New Jersey claims that arts and cultural activities pump 5.6 billion dollars a year into the economy of New York City and generate 117,000 jobs, according to a report in the *New York Times*, 16 February 1983, *Metropolitan Report* (B1), p. 1.

6. *Application Guidelines*.

7. J. Adler, 'Arts Under Reagan's Ax,' *Newsweek*, 16 March 1981, p. 28.

8. Jim Hoberman, 'Artists: An Endangered Species—Film, Video,' *Village Voice*, 13–19 May 1981, p. 41.

9. Nathan Johnson, 'Is Business the Arts' White Knight?', *Saturday Review* (July 1981), pp. 43-45.

10. Richard Goldstein, 'Artists: An Endangered Species—Let Them Eat Aesthetics,' *Village Voice*, 13–19 May 1981, pp. 39-40.

11. J A. Harris, 'While You're Up, Get Me a Grant!' *Reader's Digest* (June 1981), pp. 169-170.

12. Amos Vogel, 'Amos Vogel and Bruce Connor: Two Views of the Money Crunch,' and 'Bruce Connor Interviewed by Mitch Tuchman,' *Film Comment*, vol. 17, no. 5 (1981), pp. 70 76.

13. Richard Goldstein, 'A James Watt for the Arts?', *Village Voice*, 10-16 February 1982, p. 47.

Cinema and the Superego

Andrew Tyndall

The May 3, 1981, march in Washington, D.C. organized by the People's Anti-War Mobilization was the largest mass demonstration held by the left in this country since the end of the Vietnam war. The march was called in solidarity with the national liberation struggle in El Salvador and in opposition to U.S. intervention in favor of the ruling junta. Organizing the demonstration around this particular issue was a deliberate decision by the Marxist-Leninist groups who did the groundwork for the march. Their strategy was to build as broadly based a coalition as possible as quickly as possible in opposition to a whole range of Reagan administration policies.

The El Salvador struggle was chosen because it was sufficiently far from home to function as a representation for the specific domestic struggles being waged by the groups intended to form the base for this broad coalition. The line of march turned out to be a veritable montage of these representations:

> Just as black children are being murdered in Atlanta, so peasants are being murdered in El Salvador.

> Just as poor women are being forced to be sterilized, so El Salvador is being made barren.

> Just as inner cities are being devastated by Reagan's cuts in the domestic budget, so El Salvador is being devastated by Reagan's increases in the defense budget.

> Just as Christian peace is destroyed here, so Christian nuns are destroyed there.

> Just as nuclear power will lay waste to our land, so military power will lay waste to their land.

Just as the sexual desire of homosexuals is countered by oppression, so the political desire of the Salvadoran people is countered by oppression.

Just as this country's youth is threatened with a U.S. military draft, so El Salvador's guerrillas are threatened with a U.S. military intervention.

Just as men rape women, so the U.S. rapes El Salvador.

Just as workers here need unions to make gains from their bosses, so the peasants in El Salvador need to unite to take land from their landlords.

This diversity shows the success of the demonstration. The tactic was to bring together the contradictory elements of a leftist coalition as early as possible in the building of an anti-Reagan movement, rather than to fall into the trap of the 1960s and early 70s. At that time the tendency was to let sleeping contradictions lie, which ultimately led to the separation of the anti-war movement from the black struggle, from the women's movement, from the ecologists, and so on.

The Reagan budget cuts are obviously of central concern to all those concerned with film—threatening as they do academic institutions engaged in film theory, organizations which exhibit non-Hollywood Films, and film production funds. First, how are we to protect the hard-won advances that have been made in film theory over the past ten years? And second—a point which is somewhere between important, preposterous and impertinent—how can we, as people committed to a social practice of the cinema (of some sort or another), develop that practice to contribute to the building of the left in this country?

So, I'll start from a film.

There is a scene in Laura Mulvey and Peter Wollen's film, *Amy!*, in which the heroine, the intrepid aviatrix Amy Johnson, decides to leave her old life behind and take off on a flight to Australia. I remember thinking at the time I saw the movie that this was not the most successful scene of the film, and I still think that now. But that just goes to show that the unconscious is no aesthetician. In fact, it is not interested in film criticism or in matters of taste of any kind. For the fact remains that this scene—in which Amy sits by an open fire in her living room and burns bundles of love letters from the admirer she is about to abandon—was the one that stayed with me. Or perhaps it is the one *I* stayed with.

It was only a few days later that I remembered a scene from my childhood. I was seven years old at the time and my parents were preparing to move from the home of my infancy to the home of my adolescence. It was the first week of November, the time at which English families celebrate Bonfire

Night in honor of the burning at the stake of Guy Fawkes, a saboteur who attempted to blow up the English Houses of Parliament in the early 17th-century. Because we were moving, the bonfire included the incineration of the excess accumulation of the previous five years.

All this I cannot remember. It is constructed backwards from the clear image of what I can remember—my parents throwing onto the fire bundles of love letters dating back at least ten years to their long courtship and engagement. The reason I know that the letters must have been that old is that instead of Queen Elizabeth stamps, they had King George stamps on them, the son of the King George on Amy Johnson's letters.

What did this letter-burning signify? Or what did the movement between the two houses, which this letter burning represented, signify? The answer that immediately occurred to me was that I can remember mother taking up her occupation as a doctor only after we moved to the new house. . . . A doctor, moreover, following in her mother's footsteps. . . . Her mother, a contemporary of Amy Johnson. . . . Her mother whose maiden name was Johnson.

I will resist pursuing these introspections further and content myself with a reflection. Our individual memories have a share in determining the content of a film; at the same time we start from the content of the film to build up subsequent analysis.

Or, to put it another way, it is impossible to legislate the meaning of any particular film. If we work thus individually on individual films, then the whole practice of textual analysis is brought into question. How can we do an analysis of one film outside of an actual psychoanalysis? And then every individual's analysis would necessarily be idiosyncratic. If, on the other hand, I only talk in terms of those things which are socially determined in what I saw in a given film, am I not omitting those things which for me were most important?

What am I left to discuss? Matters of taste?

All of this makes it clear that if we are to talk about films we should consider them not as texts, but in terms of how they are used. And since our problem is to develop a social practice of the cinema, we have to address the problem of how films are used socially.

This is an especially thorny problem when dealing with political films. When I went to see *9 to 5*, nothing on earth could have persuaded me that this was a political film: half-way between *Charlie's Angels* and *Alice*, it seemed tailor-made to be a trailer for a situation comedy series. It was not until weeks later that I discovered that as a consequence of the success of the film, the AFL-CIO had invited Working Women, the organization of office workers, to form a local of the service workers' union and was funding them to organize clerical workers nationwide. However, I cannot account for this political effect from the film itself. It was certainly no more populist than *Norma Rae*, which had no similar effect in spurring the AFL-CIO into action, although it was certainly as successful at the box office. *9 to 5* is justified retrospectively by the use to which it was put, just as, in different times and for different uses, *Young Mr. Lincoln* can be called a political film, justified by the use to which it was put by *Cahiers du cinéma*.

That is, a film does not stand by itself pure and simple. The work that is done on it by an individual spectator or through a discourse of criticism or by groups acting together politically can mean that at one time the same film can be useful and useless, exciting and boring, progressive and reactionary, good and bad. This is not to valorize these political films I have just mentioned, just as to talk about my childhood was not to valorize *Amy!*; it is to say that the political effectivity of a film is dependent on how it is used. And any film is more or less susceptible to political use at the right time.

So in our project—the quest for a social practice of the cinema—we have dismissed our individual activity on a film as contingent on the individual, and our political activity as contingent on our politics. We have a social practice of the cinema which leaves no room for films.

But here psychoanalysis comes to the rescue. It supplies us with an analogy we can use, then discard immediately. Just as dreams are the guardians of sleep but only a small part of the process of sleep itself, so films may be the guardians of cinema. They are necessary so that cinema does not disappear, but they are not the process of cinema itself. Having said that, we can discard any notion that films are like dreams and continue with four examples, which I quote in tribute to, with affection for, and with gratitude towards my dear friend Ivan Ward.

The first is a very simple one. It deals with the fact that we all have to pay for our pleasure. Or to put it more precisely, in order to do whatever it is we *do* do when we go to the movies, we have to enter a contract to do it, otherwise it doesn't work. This is clear from the example of film festivals, where people who would never dream of walking out on a film they had paid to see have no compunction whatsoever about walking out of a film they can see for free. To put it simply, we can't enjoy it unless we pay for it. Or to put it less simply, when we pay for it, we pay for the situation of doing it (that is, watching a film); whereas when it's free, it (that is the film) has to be good enough for its own sake.

The second example is quite ludicrous. It deals with one afternoon when a male friend and I decided that it was about time we went to see some male gay pornographic movies. I said quite confidently that I knew the movie theater; we paid our money without looking at the marquee, and sat down in the auditorium, an auditorium I can best describe as steamy—a crowded, smelly flea pit filled with movement and good humor. We started to watch what turned out to be decidedly heterosexual pornography. Eventually I turned around in embarrassment, not unmixed with amusement at myself, and said, 'We are in the wrong theater.'

The gay theater was on the next block. There the admission charge was $3 more, and we walked into an almost empty auditorium which smelled strongly of antiseptic. We sat down and after five minutes of extremely boring screen masturbation, my friend said he must have left his gloves in the heterosexual theater, and left to find them. While he was gone I went downstairs to the bathroom and discovered why the theater was so empty.

Eventually my friend and I reunited and muttered deploringly about the poor quality of the films we were seeing. However, after an hour or so, I looked around at him and saw him sitting there with his elbows on the arms of his seat and his fingers in his mouth. I was about to point out the contradiction between what he said about the film and how he sat, when I looked at myself and realized that I was no less subject to the same criticism . . . one hand on my crotch and busily sucking my thumb.

This example has convinced me yet again that when we watch movies, we have to have something in our mouths. And if the fire department bans cigarette smoking, that only serves to boost sales of popcorn. I intend to elaborate later on the issues of the socializing in the bathroom and cinema as a group phenomenon. Incidentally, my friend lost his gloves.

The third example has to do with the film *Popeye*, a film in which the young sailor cries himself to sleep in his hammock each night with a monologue toward an obscured portrait of his father, a man by whom he was abandoned and for whom he has been engaged in a lifelong search. When we eventually see this portrait, it contains nothing—nothing, that is, except a frame which borders the words 'Me Poppa.' His father is nothing but a sign, a sign moreover belonging to that peculiar signifying system to which we give the name language.

Another friend of mine went to see this film with her brother, a brother to whom, by all accounts, she was exceptionally close during childhood. The process of watching the film was quite complicated: it involved being reseated six separate times. The reason for this was that every time somebody came to sit behind the pair of siblings, the brother became extremely nervous and demanded that they move to another seat where no one would be behind them.

All we need say is that we always have to make a compromise between watching a movie and being watched watching it. It was not for nothing that the Drifters sang about kissing in the back row of the movies. And it certainly does not have to be illicit images that we are watching for us to know that there is something on the level of the forbidden about sitting in the dark and catching a glimpse of what is projected over our heads.

The fourth and most important example is called to mind by Freud's description of the very loose libidinous ties of members of an audience compared to believers in a church or soldiers in an army. He uses the example of a play in which the Assyrian army is told, 'The general has lost his head,' with the result that the soldiers all take flight in panic. In Freud's argument it has to be news of such calamitous nature with regard to a leader to break up a group such as an army. He argues on the other hand that an audience is not bound together in the same way with regard to a leader, and therefore functions less as a group.[1]

This reminds me of the New York blackout of 1977. At the time I was sitting in Theater 80 St. Mark's and, as usual at that theater, before the movie started, it was announced that in compliance with the fire laws of the City of New York smoking was forbidden. And, as usual, once the film started no one smoked.

When the first minor blackout occurred, the film went off and everyone thought it was a fault of the projection. We sat there and after a few minutes the film started up again. But a few minutes later, when the second, major blackout took place, a remarkable thing happened. We all, simultaneously, in the pitch-black auditorium without even an exit sign visible, lit up cigarettes.

With the film gone, the social cohesion which gave authority to the city's fire laws was gone too. A more genteel form of panic cannot be imagined. But I'm sure that anyone who was in that audience knew precisely the justification for the looting which in other parts of town accompanied the blackout. We must remind ourselves of what we are doing here at this conference: that is, looking for signposts towards a social practice of the cinema.

So . . . what is to be done?

In 1902 Lenin answered this question with a proposal which strikes us here and now as patently absurd. He said the answer was to publish a newspaper. Not another newspaper! For how many years do we have to suffer the assaults on our senses of yet more periodicals, marginally claiming our attention for this group or that? Yet I feel compelled, as we all should, to follow Lenin.

He recommended that a newspaper should be published, knowing as well as we do that its contribution to the building of a communist party would have the impact of a grain of sand hitting a skyscraper. His reason for advocating this apparently imbecilic measure was that it would be a focus around which ties within the party could be strengthened and expanded. So he realized that the publication and distribution of a newspaper was essentially a structure of networks involving the establishment of ties on which eventually other more important organizational structures could be built.

Our problem, of course, is a lot more difficult than Lenin's. All he had to do was organize a Communist Party clear-thinking and strong enough to lead the way to world revolution. Once that problem was clear in his mind, issues such as 'Towards a Social Practice of a Newspaper' could be solved without conferences and without having to consult the discourses of Foucault, Lacan, Lukács et al. We on the other hand feel the need for such conferences and such consultation. For we have a much more Promethean task: how to arrive at a project by starting from a technology, the technology of films. So let me recapitulate.

Psychoanalysis can reassure us that certain elements are central to the cinema, and we ignore those elements at our peril. First of all, the economic division in commercial movie theaters in this country involves two quite separate forms of payment, initially at the box office, then subsequently at the concession stand. The box office payment is in the nature of a contract which provides us with a position from which to look at a film in safety and without distraction. The concession stand payment is the exhibitor's source of revenue and profit which results from the need for oral gratification arising from the original contract.

Secondly, we must never forget that moviegoing is a group activity. As members of an audience we are bound together by ties of love, love for this object which is for us and for us alone. We are bound together as well by the knowledge that only as a group can we enjoy the thrill of seeing that which is forbidden without being punished for it.

Having said that let us return to the question: Which way towards a social practice of the cinema? Let us return to the question by way of a detour.

In the late 1960s Andy Warhol embarked on a project to make a film every two weeks. One of these, *I, A Man*, is composed of a series of bedside chats between its star, Tom Baker, and the woman he has supposedly just slept with. The impression is that the sex was perfunctory and slightly nauseating for both parties. The process by which the film was made was that Baker and Warhol would plan what to say beforehand, go out and pick up a suitable woman in a bar, bring her back to bedroom, place her before the camera and interrogate her. Baker has said that one of the aims of this film was to test the obscenity laws. The film was screened in small downtown movie houses in major metropolitan centers. At the time these houses were showing independent domestic productions such as Warhol's, foreign art films, avant-garde experimental films and revivals. I believe it was in cinemas such as these that Silvana Mangano's buttocks would have been on display.[2] This film and others succeeded in their challenge to the obscenity laws, and within a few years these theaters were screening a completely new genre of American independent films, namely hard-core pornography.

It has only been since then that American independent films have been screened in the series of media arts centers which have sprung up in the last ten years and which are now threatened with Reagan's budget cuts.[3]

The logic of the argument I am making here is that the ax will fall and the media arts centers will be cut off—precisely because they function to drag films out of the theater and into art. And a film without a theater is like a fish without a bicycle. It would be almost impossible to organize a powerful enough constituency to put pressure on the administration to preserve the life of such a misconceived child.

I think it to be flying in the face of how films actually work to have an institution which is committed to a social practice of the cinema yet is not showing films eight hours a day, seven days a week. It is certain that what gets people out of their homes and coming together on a regular basis to deal with films is the fact that they are being shown.

Over the past year several films have been used as sites for political organization, particularly in protest against them. Examples include films such as *Cruising, Fort Apache, the Bronx, Dressed to Kill* and *Bad Timing*, as well as groups such as Women Against Pornography. These protests raise the question of what is the role of film theory in the social practice of the cinema, specifically in exhibition practice.

Just because we at the Asilomar conference oppose the reactionary policies of the Reagan administration, we are not committed to the present type of independent film exhibition practice, which is in jeopardy because of those policies. Rather, it should be our project to develop a type of exhibition practice which could have a coherent place in the opposition to those policies as a whole.

So the exhibition practice I am proposing is not merely to start yet another movie theater. Rather I want to say that an institution committed to a social practice of the cinema cannot exist unless it is tied to theatrical exhibition. To return to an example I used earlier, such an institution could be built on the model of the cinema of gay pornography, where, to paraphrase Lenin, the exhibition of films is a structure involving the establishment of ties on which eventually more important structures could be built.

In this country, Hollywood having staked its claim to the title of national cinema, an independent cinema cannot use the protective clothing of the national to legitimize itself. Independent cinema has no choice but to be at least anti-monopolist, if not actually leftist. Independent cinema's exhibition selections have to follow the same concern for broad-based diversity, coalition building and the working through of contradiction through representation that the May 3 El Salvador march displayed.

And the way film theorists, on the defensive as academies cut back and government funds dry up, can guarantee that their work is indispensable not just within the practice of the cinema, but within wider social practices, is, as it were, to make their presence felt in the lounges of these metaphorical gay porno houses.

NOTES

1. Sigmund Freud, *Group Psychology and the Analysis of the Ego*, trans. and ed. James Strachey (New York: W.W. Norton, 1975).

2. Michael Silverman, 'Italian Film and American Capital, 1947-1951,' in this volume, p. 43.

3. Maureen Turim, 'The Retraction of State Funding of Film and Video Arts and its Effects on Future Practice,' in this volume, pp. 132-141.

4. Discussion of *Bad Timing* and *Dressed to Kill* occurred during the conference at which these papers were first presented. See the contributions of Linda Williams and Teresa de Lauretis to *Re-vision: Essays in Feminist Film Criticism*, ed. Mary Ann Doane, Patricia Mellencamp and Linda Williams (Los Angeles, CA: The American Film Institute, 1983.)